MOVING CULTURE

by Paul Willis and Team

An enquiry into the cultura

Calouste Gulbenkian Foundation, London,

Published by Calouste Gulbenkian Foundation
98 Portland Place
London W1N 4ET
Telephone 0171 636 5313

© Calouste Gulbenkian Foundation
first published 1990
reprinted 1996

ISBN 0 903319 51 9

British Library Cataloguing-in-Publication Data
A catalogue record of this book is available from the British Library

Designed by The Upper Room 0181 686 4414
Distributed by Turnaround Publisher Services Ltd 0181 829 3000

Contents

Foreword

This report is a shortened and substantially re-written version of *Common Culture*, the title given to the full report of the enquiry published by the Open University Press. While the latter takes a reflective, sociological view of its subject, this report is concerned with more pragmatic questions of policy and practice. Because they are separate publications they have been given different titles. However, both books were published on the same day.

The origins of the enquiry date back to 1987, a year when the priorities governing the Foundation's support for young people's creative activities were being deliberately extended beyond the arts in schools, where they were chiefly focused, to support for activities in a range of out-of-school settings. These included youth clubs, art centres and the variety of venues used by youth theatre and youth dance groups. Although these activities complemented the arts in the school curriculum, and provided a degree of freedom that schools were seldom able to offer, it was also apparent that they represented only a small proportion of young people's cultural interests. They were among its more formal, organised manifestations. Elsewhere, in young people's homes, in the streets, in the many places they chose to meet informally, they were continually engaged in cultural activities of their own choosing or their own making: in listening to or creating pop music, in developing their own dance styles, in experimenting with ways of dressing, and so on. If activities of this kind were not conventionally described as 'artistic' this perhaps said more about our narrow use of the term than about the nature of the activities themselves. It was clear that if the Foundation wished to develop funding priorities relevant to the creative needs of the majority of young people, and not simply the few, it would need to take these activities into account: to embrace both ends of the continuum of creative activity, the informal as well as the more formal.

The nature of these informal or everyday cultural activities, their role in young people's lives and how they might be sensitively (an important word in the present context) nourished and supported by both private and statutory bodies, is the subject of this report. We hope it will stimulate debate and, more ambitiously perhaps, encourage a re-appraisal of the way in which creative activities in the lives of young people are both regarded and supported.

Simon Richey
Assistant Director, Education
Calouste Gulbenkian Foundation, UK Branch

Author's Preface

It's a great honour and also a real pleasure for me to have been asked to direct the enquiry reported on here and to compile this report. Particularly so since I believe that my choice for this task was a bold decision for the Gulbenkian Foundation, thereby indicating that they were looking outside the arts world and its mostly unsuccessful attempts to involve young people, for new thinking on youth participation. Indeed, initially the work did seem to be something of a detour from my interests which were at that time in the general social and economic condition of youth, in youth unemployment and in youth policy questions. That is not how it's turned out. As so often happens with unplanned detours, serendipidity has proved a better guide than the maps I was trying to follow. Detour and destination have changed and conditioned each other in unexpectedly creative ways. The single main thing I have learned, or perhaps relearned, through my work for this report has been the importance of thinking through all policy questions, social and economic as well as those designated cultural or artistic, with a full appreciation of the creative cultural dimension of youth experience as outlined in the following pages. This lesson will remain with me and, I hope, with others.

The aim of this report is to record and present some of the creative cultural activities of young people's informal lives - a selection from the 'common culture' of their everyday life and embedded in their common routines.

The method of the research upon which this report is based was a loose and general form of ethnography utilising, in particular, the recorded group discussion. The spine of the enquiry was research undertaken by the full-time researcher on the project, Joyce Canaan - a recent anthropology PhD graduate from the University of Chicago. In Wolverhampton during 1987 and 1988 she taped discussions with groups of young people in a variety of places including colleges, youth clubs and mother and toddler groups. The starting point for most of these discussions was to ask the group how they spent their time, often going through a 24-hour cycle, and to ask them what things or activities most interested them during the course of a typical day. Most of the young people involved were in their late teens or early twenties, single and, generally speaking, in working class occupations or from working class backgrounds. Ample evidence from our observations shows, however, that most of the processes and practices discussed hold true as tendencies within the middle class as well as the working class and are major cultural forces for levelling out important features of different class experiences.

At the same time as the Wolverhampton research, fifteen separate commissioned studies were taking place throughout the country covering a wide range of young people's cultural activities, usually involving substantial further ethnographic work in locations ranging from Sunderland to Leicester, from South Birmingham to London. A full list of the commissioned studies appears as the Appendix to this report.

This report presents only a selection of the cultural activities of young people (*Common Culture*, published by the Open University, makes a fuller presentation of the research). There are many omissions, though our decision to focus in this report on music, the cultural media and style and fashion deliberately reflects the quantitative and qualitative importance of these things in the generality of youth activity and experience. We would claim, however, that the approach and analysis outlined could be replicated for most if not all the cultural forms and activities associated with young people.

Where not otherwise stated, quotes from young people are drawn from the Wolverhampton study except in the case of the music section which draws more on the Birmingham fieldwork conducted by Simon Jones. All names have been changed. Respondents were told that it was intended to produce a published report from our researches.

Although the report carries my name it is the result of a substantial collective enterprise. Geoff Hurd, now head of the School of Humanities and Social Sciences at Wolverhampton Polytechnic, was the assistant director of the project and throughout its course contributed ideas and suggestions including two substantial position and review papers which I've drawn on in compiling this report. Joyce Canaan wrote up the Wolverhampton study in a 40,000-word field report which this report draws upon throughout. Simon Jones drew together his own work and other work completed for the enquiry on music and on style/ fashion in two mini-reports which form the bases for those two sections in this report. Throughout the report I've drawn on different aspects of the fifteen commissioned studies. Team discussions with Geoff Hurd, Joyce Canaan and Simon Jones fed directly into the writing of the report as well as some very extended comments and suggestions for textual revision from a variety of individuals including: Phil Corrigan, Stephen Yeo, Huw Beynon, Michael Green, Celia Lury and Doug Foley. Kim Taylor, director (now retired) of the UK Branch of the Gulbenkian Foundation, and Simon Richey, an assistant director, have been unstinting in support, creative commentary and suggestion throughout the course of the enquiry but especially in its closing stages. Warm personal thanks to them. Thanks too, to Josie Wall who has shown great patience and professionalism in typing up several versions of the manuscript. Thanks also to West Midlands Arts who gave invaluable co-operation in helping to organise financial aspects of the project, and to Wolverhampton Polytechnic who were most generous in housing, servicing and supporting the project.

Most importantly, thanks to the young people whose words we use, whose activities we describe and to whose further creativity this report is dedicated.

Paul Willis, Wolverhampton, March, 1990

1 Four Essential Preliminary Notes

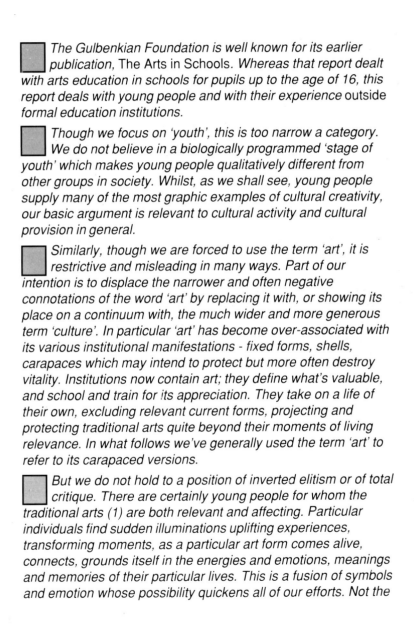

The Gulbenkian Foundation is well known for its earlier publication, The Arts in Schools. *Whereas that report dealt with arts education in schools for pupils up to the age of 16, this report deals with young people and with their experience outside formal education institutions.*

Though we focus on 'youth', this is too narrow a category. We do not believe in a biologically programmed 'stage of youth' which makes young people qualitatively different from other groups in society. Whilst, as we shall see, young people supply many of the most graphic examples of cultural creativity, our basic argument is relevant to cultural activity and cultural provision in general.

Similarly, though we are forced to use the term 'art', it is restrictive and misleading in many ways. Part of our intention is to displace the narrower and often negative connotations of the word 'art' by replacing it with, or showing its place on a continuum with, the much wider and more generous term 'culture'. In particular 'art' has become over-associated with its various institutional manifestations - fixed forms, shells, carapaces which may intend to protect but more often destroy vitality. Institutions now contain art; they define what's valuable, and school and train for its appreciation. They take on a life of their own, excluding relevant current forms, projecting and protecting traditional arts quite beyond their moments of living relevance. In what follows we've generally used the term 'art' to refer to its carapaced versions.

But we do not hold to a position of inverted elitism or of total critique. There are certainly young people for whom the traditional arts (1) are both relevant and affecting. Particular individuals find sudden illuminations uplifting experiences, transforming moments, as a particular art form comes alive, connects, grounds itself in the energies and emotions, meanings and memories of their particular lives. This is a fusion of symbols and emotion whose possibility quickens all of our efforts. Not the art itself, however, nor its carapace, but its human use and personal relevance are what make lightning contact possible between symbolic form and human condition. Our aim is not to criticise 'art' but to insist that such symbolic uses, such energising symbolic contacts, occur much more widely than is usually recognised: not the preserve of institutions, they are part of everyday and ordinary cultural experience.

(1) see Notes on page 69

2 A Different Starting Point

In our thinking about youth and the arts we must start from unpalatable truths or from no truths at all. It is 'worse' truths we need, not 'better' lies. The worst truth is that the traditional arts (1) play very little part in young people's lives.

Accepting, believing, acting on this worst truth is the only way to a better truth - 'the arts' may be dead, but not 'art in life'. For it's high time we started from where young people are rather than from where traditional arts or youth policies think they ought to be. In order to do this we need to pose *different* questions.

Not exclusively, 'how can we bring 'the arts' to youth?'
but 'in what ways are the young already in some sense the artists of their own lives?'

Not exclusively, 'why is their culture not like ours?'
but 'what are their cultures like?'

Not 'how can we inspire the young with Art?'
but 'how are the young already culturally energised in ways which we can re-inforce?'

Unlike the traditional ones, these new questions can never be asked from an armchair. We need to ask youth directly, we need to look at and observe the active contexts of their answers. We need to refuse old categories of understanding and develop new ones so that we can appreciate what we see and hear.

Our starting point, our first refusal, is in the recognition that for the majority of the young, the institutionalised and increasingly standardised arts have absolutely no place in their lives. Many have a negative view: the arts are seen as remote and institutional, the preserve of art galleries, museums and concert halls that are 'not for the likes of us'. More damaging, however, is the fact that the formal existence of arts, in the sense in which the term is commonly used, seems to deny everything else an artistic or cultural content. In other words, because Art is in the Art Gallery it can't be anywhere else. It does not belong to the lives of 'normal' people.

The emphatic preferences of the experts - persuasively defined, enshrined in museums, priced in galleries, promoted and preserved for posterity in institutions - have so far told us what is 'Art' and what is not. If, as is manifestly the case, these are adult enterprises, so too are their audiences. As a recent *Cultural Trends* (2) publication points out, the audiences for the traditional performing arts have shown remarkable consistency over several decades right up to the present, we might call them the 'the 3-M audience' - middle class, middle-aged and minority. The *1986 General Household Survey* suggests that only 5% of the population regularly attends the 'theatre/ballet/opera' and 4% 'museums/art galleries'. Only 2% of the working class attends any of these. These figures have not varied over the last ten years of the coverage of the *General Household Survey* (2). The work conducted in 1983 for *The Youth Review* (3) suggests that the most popular of the traditional arts venues, the theatre, attracts (excluding students) something under 2% of young people (up to 23 years of age) with zero attendance for the young unemployed.

However, if the term 'arts' is given an altogether wider definition, then it will be seen that life is full of expressions, signs and symbols through which individuals and groups creatively establish their very presence, as well as important elements of their identity, purpose and meaning. Young people are all the time expressing, or struggling to express, something of their own - or their hoped for - *cultural significance*. It is this which must be grasped and extended - not an attempt to circulate more widely the keys to the museum or cheaper tickets for the opera.

We believe that our best chances of encouraging an artistic democracy are not through 'democratisation' of 'the arts' - opening access for new 'publics' to the established institutions and practice - but through an identification, recognition and support of existing creative experiences and activities not at present regarded as 'artistic' but which are now part of our common culture. We are thinking of a wide range of creative activities and forms of expression and communication young people find relevant to their lives - fashion and pop music, room and personal decoration, the rituals of romance, subcultural group styles, magazines, radio and television. The key shift here is to change from a narrow focus on 'art' to a much wider concern with the common culture of the young. Or to put it another way, the boundaries drawn between arts and non-arts need to be re-drawn or declared entirely defunct. We need a view which accepts a continuum of expressive forms, practices, resources and materials through which the young symbolically portray their meanings, which they press into play as symbolic languages for the expression and formation of their identities.

Our report aims to make a reversal in what seems to have become the accepted chain of logic in our society - that participation in 'Art' produces 'Culture' (for the few). A comparative or historical view readily grants that different cultures produce different arts. But this awareness has worn very thin in our everyday sense of our own culture. We aim to rehabilitate this awareness and to install it at the centre of policy debate. We need to say again that cultures are intertwined with, and produce, everyday forms of art, only a small part of which is ever recognised as 'Art'.

But under contemporary conditions this broad field of common culture is usually seen simply as 'mass culture' and its bastard child, 'youth culture'. Both imply problems and pathologies, deviations and disturbances. They are both about exploitation, or the degradation or displacement of authentic artistic culture, of 'cultured' culture. These definitions and attitudes need turning inside out and upside down.

It is evident that most of the common cultural experience of young people takes place through provided commercial forms - the cultural media and cultural commodities provided for profit, and now increasingly internationally organised. The cultural industries provide products (songs, clothes, films, programmes) in order to *appeal* in any and every possible way, and thereby to sell, rather than to improve or educate. They are manufactured in rationalised production systems comparable in most respects to the factory production of consumer products in general. Stunningly different texts and songs, wildly heterogeneous appearances and images jostle each other in the market place. Divisions of time and space, essential to and imprinted on the production of commodities, seem to dissolve in boundless invitations to their consumption. Revivals vie with imports. Manifestations from every culture, however close or distant, become permanent and transmissable, instant and contemporary.

The usual conclusion drawn from these evident truths, namely that young people are manipulated and dominated by commercial culture, is simplistic and unwarranted. By definition the market is anarchic. Marketeers and marketing are in a continuing crisis precisely because the (especially young) consumers are moving all the time. Market categories and boundaries have become completely unstable (especially youth categories), and it is virtually impossible now to predict future patterns of taste (especially youthful taste). Shorter product development cycle times and larger concentrations of resources in ever bigger conglomerates are in part commercial responses attempting to limit this uncertainty, as well as likely future casualties of it. But it can't be had both ways. The cultural industries in helter-skelter growth and anarchy are hardly in any shape to dominate and plan their own consciousness and future, never mind those of ranks of refractory and restless youth.

Let us say then, categorically, that youth's rejection of, or lack of interest in, 'art' does not mean automatic subjection to 'mass culture'. Rather, the cultural industries should be understood as providing the symbolic resources - fronting the only cultural world which most young people know - within and out of which youth experience, identity and expression are creatively fashioned.

For young people it is not the commercialisation and commodification of culture *per se* which is the problem. On the contrary, it is clear that the market has been a liberating factor in the extension of the cultural resources for many young people. In fact young people have a creative role in shaping the contours of commercial culture in ways which are quite forbidden to them within 'official cultures'- education, literature, the arts - where the combined forces of privilege, class and the state too often reduce young people to powerless subjects. On the contrary, the market defines the geography of young people's culture. It is that world which they are taking over, transforming, and turning into real youth art.

These heresies and claims may seem unlikely. How can the flotsam and jetsam of the market be promoted into new art? The problem here is that adults, educators and commentators have taken the commodities of the market place at face value, at a surface and atomised valuation unconnected with practice and context. It's true that many cultural commodities are ephemeral, insubstantial, changing, changeable - aimed at making people purchase through surface appeal. They're aimed at exchange. But this very exchange implies *use* and common, profane everyday relevance in and to normal activity - the very thing that the arts or their institutions have forbidden. By contrast, the market for cultural forms and services *depends* on its products being taken up and given meaning within the informal social relations of young people's lives. That is why marketing culture is not a simple business or a matter of manipulation - young people must be involved in shaping the contours of commercial culture through the *uses* they make of its products. And it is those uses which contain the promise and the creativity - the hidden continent of symbolic work and creativity which is forming real identities and energising skills, awakening sensuous capacities every day.

We accept that being addressed as consumers by the cultural industries and exercising a symbolic creativity through their products is not a cultural empowerment in anything like a full sense, but it is nevertheless an empowerment which has not been offered elsewhere. It may not be the best way to cultural emancipation for the majority, but it may open up the way to a better way. Only through some creative control and the exercise *through use* - however done and through whatever materials - of symbolic faculties and capacities will new demands and new levels of control and mastery be made possible at all.

Simplistic notions of 'consumer sovereignty' are no more relevant here than the pessimistic litany of manipulation, pacification and incorporation. These positions tell us everything about the speaker and nothing about living culture. The materials of popular culture may or may not be formularistic, contrived and banal, but they do provide usable symbolic resources for common cultural activities on a far larger scale than has been the case before. It is the *uses* of these cultural materials, not their surface forms, which we want to capture, to hold and move on from.

3 Grounded Aesthetics

We have deliberately retrieved the term 'aesthetic' from its conventional stronghold to emphasise the positive side of the practical and sensuous *creative uses* of everyday cultural resources. We'll use it to reframe and represent 'mundane', 'degraded' or 'commercial' materials from the point of view of their creative use in human *activity*. This may, of course, outrage those who wish reverentially to reserve the term for the careful handling of the special, heightened and precious within safe artistic temples. But other societies, earlier civilisations, 'less developed' cultures have also revelled in a rumbustious, robust and profane vesting and testing of aesthetics in the everyday. So does ours if only we will look.

Our addition of 'grounded' to the traditional term aims to convey some sense of scepticism about the 'flight' of conventional aesthetics. Too often this renders the once socially relevant and once serious effects of art, once passionately felt and understood, into the sublime entertainment of a purely formal aesthetic response to, for instance, religious art now installed in the antiseptic stillness of the museum. We want to bring aesthetics back to earth - not for a crash landing, but to give them opportunities to show their worth in the 'earthiness' of the normal conditions of everyday life.

In amongst the plethora of expressions which help to constitute the different cultural fields of the young are some which are made to 'come alive' to some degree: a particular pop song suddenly evoking and coming to represent an intense personal episode or experience; a dramatic situation in a soap opera paralleling and illuminating dilemmas and problems in the family, with friends, or at school or college; a look in a fashion magazine sparking new ideas for personal style and adornment. Such items can be symbolically appropriated to produce a cutting edge of meaning which not only reflects or repeats what exists, but creatively transforms what exists - previous personal experience and hopes for the future being reorganised, made more understandable or handleable; externally provided expressions changed by being made to signify in new personally 'significant' ways. Thus charged, both experience and representation can further change, interact and develop through processes of creative consumption, creative perception and re-perception. In this way the received world is made human and, to however small a degree, controllable.

The possibility of such control is, of course, a collective principle for the possibility of political action on a larger scale. But it also has importance, we argue, in the individual and collective awareness of the ability to control symbols and their cultural work. In so called 'primitive art', for instance, a central theme is the naming of fundamental forces as gods and demons thereby to reveal them, make them somehow knowable and therefore subject to human persuasion or placation. Of course the urban industrial world seems much more complex in its organisation than are 'primitive' societies, and our apparent technical control over the threatening forces of nature seems greater and different in kind from theirs. What we seek to control, persuade or humanise through symbols and expressions may be, in part, the force and expression of other human beings rather than forces emanating directly from nature - if you like the work of culture on culture. Whatever the complexity of working through its applications, the point is essentially a simple one. To be crude: that to know the cultural world and our place within it, it is necessary to do more than passively exist within it and receive its offerings. For the achievement of cultural identity we must change the cultural world - however minutely. We must make of it a personalised cultural map - *these* musics, films, fashions, images, styles - which locates and helps to define personal identity and its difficulties and possibilities under modern conditions. It is the practical activity of this cultural *work* (quite literally) which we wish to hold and highlight as an everyday accomplishment in our notion of the grounded aesthetics of common culture.

This cultural work may involve no texts or artefacts, no 'artistic things' at all. There is, for instance, a dramaturgy and poetics of everyday life, of social presence, encounter and event. It may be invisible in the routinised roles of adult life, but the young have much more time and they face each other with fewer or more brittle masks. They are the practical existentialists. Inescapably, sometimes excessively, they live in the moment. For them some features of social life may not be about the regulation and containment of tension, but about its creation and increase. The 'aimless' life of groups and gangs may be about producing something from nothing, from 'doing nothing'. It may be about building tensions, orchestrating and shaping their release and further build-ups, so that a final 'catharsis' takes with it or changes other tensions and stresses inherent in the difficulties of their condition. Making a pattern in an induced swirl of events can bring moments of transcendence or transformation - strangely still centres of heightened awareness, the holding of time, control and insight. It may also be that the grounded aesthetics of, for instance, crowds, public spectacle and sports events may draw on, or parallel, the immanent dramatics of social life itself.

Of course there may well be a privileged role for texts and artefacts, not in their own inherent aesthetics but in the social possibility they offer through forms of *creative consumption*. The received view of aesthetics suggests that the aesthetic effect is internal to the text, and a universal property of its form. This places the creative impulse squarely on the material productions of the 'creative' artist, with the reception or consumption of art wholly determined by its aesthetic form - palely reflecting what is timelessly coded within the text. But the emphasis of *grounded* in our grounded aesthetics is to recognise the creativity of common culture including the creativities of apparently passive consumption.

Let us emphasise: circumstances change cases, contexts change texts. When there is nothing new in the world, a changed context is as good as a new text. We are interested to explore both how far 'meanings' and 'effects' can change quite decisively according to the social contexts of 'consumption', and the extent viewers, listeners and readers bring their own symbolic work and creativity to a text, or create their own relationships to technical means of reproduction and transfer. The creative reception of, and work on, texts and artefacts can be seen as a kind of production in its own right. But it is also part of a social process which may include its own productions - either of new forms or of combinations of existing ones. Perhaps we should see the 'raw materials' of cultural life, of communications and expressions, as always intermediate. They are the products of one process as well as the raw materials for another - whose results are raw materials for successive groups. The law of copyright recognises that every time an artefact changes form or content a new product is created on which copyright can be established. Where is our cultural realisation of this principle? Why shouldn't bedroom decoration and personal styles as combinations of the productions of others, as well as creative writing or song and music composition, be recognised as fields of aesthetic realisation? Furthermore, the grounded appropriation of new technology and new hardware may open new possibilities for expression, or re-combinations of old ones, in a way which the dominant or official culture has missed with its gaze fixed firmly on the 'things' of the past.

There are some other important ways in which grounded or everyday aesthetics differ from conventional aesthetics. The received sense of the 'aesthetic' emphasises the cerebral. At times it seems to verge on the 'an-aesthetic' - the suppression of all senses. Part of the meaning of 'grounded' is to pull the term back (actually onto its original terrain, its Greek root, aesthesis, meaning sensation) into some direct relation to the senses and to sensual heightening. The ways in which the senses are used to control - indeed 'to be' - the body as a medium of expression provides a specific and privileged case. Questions of 'economy' and 'usefulness' and 'skill' all enter into the grounded aesthetic of how the body is used. Bodily aesthetics include personal style and presence as well as dance and perhaps large areas of music and performance.

The traditional view of the aesthetic can be profoundly ascetic. Joy, pleasure and 'fun' can be equated with 'the common and the vulgar', with a necessary coarseness of form. We insist on features of pleasure and desire, whether collective or individual, which are 'fun' but also work through aspects of everyday and grounded aesthetics to give human meaning and control. Group events, performances, carnivals, parties may all figure here.

Conventional aesthetics seem usually to concern abstract or sublimated qualities of beauty - essentially Platonic notions where 'beauty' exists somewhere else, on its own, casting shapes and shadows which we fleetingly recognise in our own world. This view can be inherently anti-democratic since some can 'see' what is beautiful better than others, and so deserve reverence and special treatment. Against this, and very importantly, we see grounded aesthetics as having common everyday *uses* rather than rare and abstract value.

Usefulness has been forgotten in our sense of art as things in galleries and in our sense of past as museum - institutions devoted to translating artefacts from their useful, meaningful contexts to artificial places foreign in place, time and philosophy. The uses of grounded aesthetics may be concrete and practical, or cognitive i.e. grounded aesthetics as useful to 'think with'. Grounded aesthetics may produce meanings, explanations and pay-offs in relation to concrete conditions and situations which seem more efficient or adequate, perhaps, than other proffered meanings. Such 'useful' meanings may well have moral dimensions in providing collective and personal principles of action, co-operation, solidarity, distinction or resistance. 'Useful' meanings may also relate to difficulties and dilemmas in the realms of necessity - school, work, college - as well as to choices in the realms of leisure and free time.

There are, perhaps especially, private symbolic and expressive therapies for the injuries of life. Musical, literary or philosophical forms may be useful here not because of their intrinsic aesthetics, but because of their capacity to produce meanings and understandings which were not there before. This may involve internal, imaginative and spiritual life-prayers even for the unbeliever. It may be in the realm of dream and fantasy, in the realm of heightened awareness of the constructedness and constructiveness of the self; alienation from obvious givens and values; the sense of a future made in the present so that it changes the present; the fear of and fascination with the 'terra incognita' of the self. The work of grounded aesthetics may be in the holding and repairing (though meaning-making, creation and control, even in desperate seas) of the precariousness and fragmentedness of identity whose source of disturbance is outside, structural and beyond the practical scope of individuals to influence.

4 Music

Popular music is tremendously important for the play and generation of everyday aesthetics amongst young people. But a number of deep-rooted assumptions about the arts prevent this recognition. Music performance is regarded as 'creative' and consumption as 'passive'. In most writing about the arts this distinction between production and consumption, amateur and professional, is taken for granted as a matter of individual skill, talent and creativity.

Within popular music, and within young people's own musical practices, however, such distinctions are a good deal less clear cut. The play of everyday aesthetics bridges them. The special relationship between production and consumption in popular music culture means that most pop musicians begin as 'fans', and 'create' by copying sounds from records and cassettes - they become 'producers as consumers'.

This consumer/apprentice way of learning can be seen as the *normal* way of 'learning art' certainly pre 'the Academy' and before written notation, as well as in all folk societies and folk arts. The rigid and hierarchical distinction between production and consumption is the historical aberration, not the norm. In not yet properly recognised ways, recorded and very widely 'media-ted' music is producing a new kind of contemporary 'folk art' - this time, however, beyond and on the future side of commoditisation.

Most musical activity, then, begins as and from consumption, from the process of listening to music. The use of passive terms - audiences, consumption, reception has made us think of looking and listening as passive terms, just as, more widely, the domination of 'text' makes all cultural production equate to 'reading', usually silent. But consumption itself is creative. The cultural meaning of a song isn't hermetically sealed: it depends on consumer abilities to make value judgements, to talk knowledgeably and passionately about their genre tastes, to place music in their lives by using commodities and symbols for their own imaginative purposes. These processes involve the exercise of critical choices and uses which disrupt the taste categories and 'ideal' modes of consumption promoted by the leisure industry, and break up its superimposed definitions of musical meaning. To describe pop as 'passive' is to ignore these vital cultural processes.

For it is as important to understand how consumers' discriminating abilities are learnt and sustained as it is to discover why, in some circumstances, young pop fans become committed to performing for themselves.

For many young people buying records and tapes is an important sphere of cultural activity in itself, one that can range from casual browsing to earnest searching for particular records. It is a process that involves clear symbolic work: complex and careful exercises of choice from the point of initial listening to seeking out handling and scrutinising records.

With the prohibitive price of new records and software such as CDs, second-hand records have acquired an even greater importance for many young people. They will spend hours browsing in second-hand record stores, looking for bargains and especially for 'oldies' and 'revives'. Indeed, one of the prominent features of young people's current musical activities is their interest in 'old' music, such as 50s rock'n'roll, 60s dance music, 70s soul.

This interest in 'old' music is partly a result of record company strategies to make more revenue out of back catalogues, through re-releases, licensing songs for use in adverts, and releasing 'oldies' and 'greatest hits' compilations. But it also signals an enthusiastic interest in popular music from the 50s, 60s and 70s amongst a generation who didn't hear such music the first time round, and for whom it is in many senses 'new' and, for some, more 'authentic' than current styles. The result is that large numbers of young people now do their own archaeologies of popular music history carefully excavating the 'originals' and tracing the genealogies of particular styles, whether from films, TV clips, magazines, or re-releases. In certain club-based dance cultures, musical styles, such as those of 70s soul and disco, have been excavated and re-appropriated as dance music. This can extend into an avid collecting of old music, scouring second-hand shops for records that can be sold, swapped for others, used for the purposes of 'mixing' live in clubs or for compiling personal tapes. There is a high exchange rate of records both new and second-hand between young people, with albums and singles being swapped and borrowed regularly. These are sure signs that the interest in 'vinyl', where it can be acquired cheaply, is still alive amongst some young people.

There has also been a massive growth in home-taping. With many young people unable to afford on a regular basis full-priced new records, let alone CDs, cassette tapes have become one of the principal currencies of consumption. Records are increasingly borrowed to be taped, with some young people collecting large stores of tapes not only of records but also of live dances, gigs, parties and other musical events.

Taping music from the radio is now widespread amongst the young. Young listeners select their favourite records from the weekly chart run-down and compile their own personal *Pick of the Pops*. Alternatively, they tape new, unavailable, or expensive import records (particularly off pirate radio). By skilful manipulation of the pause button on a cassette recorder and deft cuing and rewinding, they can instantly edit out the spoken interruptions of the DJ, or jingles and commercials.

John: If I haven't got a record I'll tape it off the radio, and before the DJ starts talking, fade it down. Or new records that friends have got, I'll just tape.

With cheap twin-deck cassette recorders now widely available it is also possible to make duplicate copies of tapes themselves, and distribute them informally amongst friends for private consumption or, illegally and therefore at risk because copyright and other rights are likely to be breached, to sell them.

For those who can't afford to buy records, or who don't want to bother with the problems of consumption and choice, home-taping is an appropriate solution. This is especially so for young people who own a portable cassette player/radio, but don't have the facilities to record records. Young people frequently rely on friends to make tapes for them. An informal hierarchy of taste operates here, with the more committed and avid record collectors used as trusted and accepted 'consumer guides' by some young people; others request a particular form or style of music (slow-sentimental, uptempo-dance, roots-political) and let the tape compiler select the specific records. This process was amply demonstrated by Mary in Wolverhampton.

If I want a tape done now, all I do is buy my tape and give it to someone else to tape it for me...and I say 'Will you do this for me?', and they say 'What do you want?', and you tell them what sort of record you want. If they've got it, they'll do it, or if they've got something else different you say, 'OK fair enough, do it for me'...They'll do it for you as long as you've got the tape, but if you haven't got the tape you say 'OK, here's the money you get a tape and you do it for me, whatever change is left you can keep it'.

In this way cassette tapes enable people to make their own personal 'soundtracks' and compilations. Some young people extend this practice to experimenting with their own 'mastermixes' of dance records, the aim being to mix several records together on a tape in a continous flow, keeping, for instance the same beat, or to create interesting juxtapositions of songs, rhythms and melodies.

Songs have meaning for young people not only through their words, but also as structures of sound with unique rhythms, textures and forms. The sound of a voice, and all the extra-linguistic devices used by singers, such as vocal inflections, nuances, hesitations, emphases or sighs, are just as important in conveying meaning as explicit statements, messages and stories.

Much popular music produces 'feelings' and emotions first and foremost, before it produces any specific attitudes or forms of social consciousness; feelings of happiness/sadness, romance, sexual feelings, or uplifting feelings. In this sense the power of a particular song lies in its capacity to capture a particular 'mood' or sentiment by a complex combination of different sounds and signifying elements. As one young man said, songs could, in this way, both express intimate personal feelings and communicate them to others.

Sometimes when I want to express something I can say to a person 'Listen to this record - that's the way I'm feeling'.

Songs can be used to cope with, manage and make bearable the experiences of everyday life. Perhaps the most extreme example of this is the use of the personal stereo or Walkman, the ultimate artefact in providing a personal soundscape that can be carried around, quite literally, inside the head, while travelling, walking, waiting or negotiating public spaces. One young man, who at one stage was never to be seen without a Walkman, said that music was absolutely vital to surviving and getting through the day.

You see this tape and earphones round my neck...you know...Must have music, man!...I'd die without music!

For many young people, the syncopations and textures of dance music, through its complex polyrhythms and drum and bass patterns, have the ability to produce sensual pleasure in literally moving the body, both physically and emotionally.

June: It's heart music...music of the heart, it just gets you right there (lays her hand on her chest)...Reggae's like a heartbeat, it's the same kind of rhythm, there's something very crucial about rhythm...I'm not sure what it is.

Pete: It gets you in the gut like...Most times I don't listen to the singing. The singing's going on and that, but I listen to the bass.

Dancing is the principal way in which musical pleasures become realised in physical movement and bodily grounded aesthetics. The sensual appeal of popular music is at its greatest in dance music, where its direct courting of sexuality generates a heightened sense of self and body. Experimentation with dance styles involves its own characteristic forms of cultural work and informal, learning processes. Patrick regularly practises and rehearses routines at home, dancing to records with his brother.

You just stick a record on, and get into the groove kind of thing, like we'll work out some new moves over the weekend, and go up to the Powerhouse on a Monday and try them out like, you know...and sometimes you'll get a whole line of people doing it...It's really good.

Amongst white youth many dance styles are initially appropriated and popularised from black youth culture. Imported from America in the case of soul, funk and hip-hop, or Jamaica in the case of reggae, they are taken up by young blacks and rapidly transmitted to young whites who incorporate them into their own repertoires of cultural expression.

John: That fascinated me, and ever since then I've loved skanking. I picked up on it real fast and I'd practise the moves at home while I'm listening to my records, right. And we'd sort of mess around, me, my sister and my cousin... And they'd show me the dances they were learning.

Out of the vast numbers of young people who participate in dancing regularly, whether in clubs, pub discos or house parties, there is a sizeable group of 'serious' dancers who concentrate on and even formalise a bodily grounded aesthetic of their own. For this group the quality of a particular venue and its sound system, the individual DJ, and particularly the music policy, are extremely important. The emphasis is strictly on dancing, sometimes to the exclusion of drinking or even courting. Young people, particularly the unemployed, will often go to a club with no more than the price of admission, their nightbus fare home and perhaps enough money for one drink.

'All-dayers' are often a focal point for 'serious' dancing and are something of a speciality in the North and the Midlands. Held in particular night clubs, often on a Sunday, they regularly draw crowds of around 2,000 people who converge on the venue from as far afield as London and the South East. These are dance marathons which run for a mammoth 9 or 10 hours, and where a host of different DJs play a mixed diet of funk, soul, house music, hip-hop, Latin and jazz.

In recent years there has been diversification in music policy in some city-centre entertainment networks. In order to stay in business many clubs and discos have had to hire out their facilities to one-off 'specialist' agents, or open their doors to particular musical taste groups (punk/new wave, heavy metal, soul/funk, reggae) on particular nights of the week. One consequence of this change in policy is that club-goers and DJs have been able to create their own musical and stylistic categories and admission policies.

The more serious young dancers invest considerable work and training in their dancing routines. Two young Afro-Caribbean dancers from Walsall, for example, spoke about how they had learnt to breakdance by practising to a drum machine at home in front of a mirror.

*A lot of us train before we come out of the house, don't we?
I always do. If I know I'm on tonight I'm always stretching in
the day. I always stretch every day, bend your back up and
everything, handstand against the wall. You have to loosen
your arms and loosen your body first and you've got to move
your arms up and across sort of thing, and get it down your
body. (Ignition/Young at Art, p. 14)*

With their often elaborate and sophisticated moves, these worked up forms of popular dance have their own artistic criteria for those who practise them, criteria of originality, wit and flexibility. Amongst some young dance 'crews' (informal teams of dancers) their routine had become a kind of mime with clearly apparent narratives to them.

*There's a few teams, right, they're really breakers but
they're mainly acting. They go on stage, they do a few
dance moves but what they're actually doing is acting,
there's a story behind it all. So they do a few moves and
they leave the audience to fill in the rest. (Ignition/Young at
Art, p.14)*

As we argued before, in the contemporary folk art of popular music, young people's interest in music-making and performance invariably begins from their activities as consumers, fans and dancers, and from the everyday aesthetics and pleasures of listening to and liking particular styles of music. For example, Kevin's interest in music-making came about as an 'extension' of listening to records, dancing in night clubs and being 'inspired' by his favourite bands.

*I've always been interested in music. I've got loads of
records, I always did buy music, and I used to dance a
lot...That's got a lot to do with it you see...So the music was
just an extension of that, 'cos I always wanted to know, you
know, how they did it, or what they did to make people move
sort of thing...So then I started experimenting, started doing
things with music, just messing about...*

Kevin subsequently bought a synthesiser and learnt to play it by trying to copy his favourite records.

*The funny thing about it was the sounds that they were
using were similar to the sounds I was getting on the
machine. So I thought that's amazing! I can actually do it,*

you know. And once you can actually play along with the melody, and work it out, it's just so good, you know what I mean?

The sense of empowerment achieved by being able to play an instrument and reproduce the sounds of a favourite record is a common starting point for young musicians. To learn by copying and experimenting (the usual method for young rock musicians) is necessarily to be inventive. Guitarists, drummers and keyboard players have to work out how to sound like their role models, usually with quite different (and much cheaper) sound equipment. This means developing manual and technical skills, a discriminating ear, and an ad hoc understanding of sound amplification. As Kevin pointed out,

I was never taught or anything. Everything I do is by ear...it's all what I feel or what I've heard. I mean some people I MUSICMUSICknow, they've been taught and all that, and they're really good sort of thing, but they can't improvise, they find it difficult to sort of, you know, do anything themselves, rather than sort of have a piece of music in front of them, and playing it.

Amongst young rock musicians there is only a short gap between picking up an instrument and playing in a band, and the learning process is as much a result of practising, rehearsing and jamming together as it is of any prior, individual training and skill acquisition. Most rock bands compose their own music through informal musical procedures which bring into play grounded aesthetics to indicate what sounds good, and how to generate an effect. Because rock musicians don't read music they have to learn to play together in endless collective experiments through hours spent rehearsing together. In Kevin's band, for example, song-writing invariably evolved out of such improvised jamming sessions.

Usually, we'd just jam, then if we'd get a really nice section, we'd sort of say 'Oh that was good, let's try that again, we'll do that twice' and then we'd do that part, and cut other bits out, and try and string it together like. And as for words, and stuff like that, it wasn't sort of a session where everyone was sort of sat round, and sort of writ a song. It was more like 'eh, try singing this, this sounds alright!', or 'try this', you know what I mean, so it was just done there and then sort of thing.

For virtually all young rock bands live performance is the focal point of their work. As many young musicians explain, it is in performance that they experience the most intense feelings of achievement. To be on stage is to be the object of public attention, and to have the glamour of their chosen musical role confirmed. Kevin felt that each one of the gigs that they'd played live was a 'great occasion'.

It was all really good. 'Cos we was all young, and really into the idea of the band, kind of thing, and everything was for the band, and we were all together, like...we just had a really good time.

Musical performance, then, in this wider sense, amounts to an important expression and celebration of sociability through some shared sense of everyday aesthetics. It is inherently a collective activity. Musicians know that personal fulfilment depends on the ability to do things together, whether learning to listen and adjust to other players in the band, or evolving informal attempts at collective organisation, decision-making and financial management. For example they club together to buy equipment or hold regular 'band meetings'. In describing performance as their most satisfying musical experience, young musicians are describing a kind of collective experience which involves the audience too. When a rock show works it is because, in speaking to the crowd the musicians come to speak for them: the music both creates and articulates the very idea of a symbolically creative community.

This section has illustrated how the usually separately understood processes of musical production and consumption are closely related. The distinctions between them are blurred in musical practice, particularly around new musical technologies of consumption and production, and new symbolic uses of musical commodities. Consumption is itself a kind of self-creation - of identities, of space, of cultural forms - with its own kinds of cultural empowerment.

These forms of creative consumption around popular music point to a continuum between the more worked-up forms of musical activity and the popular practices engaged in by the young. If it's more 'producers' we want, then instead of concentrating on identifying and promoting creative elites or potential elites, we should, instead, focus on a general lubrication of the connections between these everyday forms of musical and cultural activity and the more formally recognised practices, to make the passage from the role of 'consumer' to that of 'producer' easier.

5 The Cultural Media

Television has become a pervasive part of the cultural and symbolic life of young people. Surveys of young peoples' spare time show that along with listening to the radio and playing records and tapes, watching television is the universal leisure activity. The peak periods for watching are either side of the times when young people are most likely to be out of the house: the early evening (between 5 pm and 7 pm) and the late evening. Though going out doesn't necessarily mean no television. Pubs, for example, often have sets behind the bar, sometimes tuned to one of the new satellite delivered stations like the rock music channel, MTV.

The pervasiveness of television in young peoples' lives has prompted worries about its ill effects, much of this is based on a view of the youthful audience as passive, uncreative recipients of 'messages' that enter their consciousness from outside - like a drug injected in a vein - causing altered behaviour and thinking. This view, however, is comprehensively contradicted by recent research that observed people watching television in their own homes rather than in a laboratory, and talked to them at length about their feelings and responses, allowing them to speak in their own way, without reducing their answers to ticks on a questionnaire.

The study conducted by Peter Collet of Oxford University which filmed people watching television and recorded their comments using equipment concealed in the television cabinet, provides a particularly revealing picture of everyday viewing. The tapes showed that people only have their eyes on the screen for two-thirds of the time they are in the room. The rest of the time they are reading the newspaper, dozing, and doing a variety of other things. And when they are watching they are far from passive: they shout back at the screen, make sarcastic comments about people's hair styles and dress sense, sing along with the advertising jingles and talk about the programmes while they are still on. Far from being the passive watchers of political mythology, they actively collaborate with the screen to create and recreate a web of meanings that are relevant to them and anchored in their own lives. They develop active and varied relationships with the TV screen and creatively and selectively take up its meanings and messages. They develop their own everyday aesthetics in forms of creative consumption.

From our fieldwork it is clear that TV is omnipresent in daily life - 'whether we'm watching or not, it's buzzing in the background'; 'it's just more homely when I have it on in the kitchen'. It can also be a foreground - 'you tend to be able to make good conversation out of it'. But there are no 'automatic effects' from the TV on young peoples' lives or perceptions. Young people especially, actively control where and how TV functions in their own landscape. They are highly tele-literate in interpreting sounds and images and taking them up into their own grounded symbolic work and meanings.

There is widespread familiarity with and understanding of different conventions, stereotypes and TV genres: 'comedy ain't meant to be realistic, it's meant to make you laugh'; '*Eastenders*, you know what to expect before it happens'; 'They portray black women to be big, big busted and big butts and fat'; 'Excitement, money...getting involved in the quizzes and questions they ask, guessing the answer before they say'; 'American soaps exaggerate the good points and ours exaggerate the bad points'. As these quotes show, there is an everyday aesthetic in simply identifying how the different conventions invite you to play a role and in deciding how to respond to them - far from a 'passive' activity, even if someone else is defining the roles.

It is true that most television was judged in our discussion groups by criteria relating to realism. But this does not imply interpretive laziness or vulnerability to realist 'ideologies'. The exercise of realist criteria requires the active work of comparison and, ironically and contradictorily, a full working knowledge of the difference between reality and representation. This is precisely about an ability to separate and recombine representation and reality. Generally young people do not mistake fiction for reality. Rather the reverse, they understand that it's the reality behind how the shows are made which helps to determine their form and quality as 'realistic' representations.

JC: Do you like Dallas?

Sandra: I liked it at the beginning, but then I think it went down a bit. I think it went down since it came back. The part that ruined it was when Pam was having that dream about how Bobby got killed or something like that, I think it got ruined then.

Margaret: It was a bit stupid...fantasy. But they had to do that because these top actors, right, they decided they were gonna quit the place, the film, and when they got offered more money, they got back into it.

Comparative tastes are clear and evaluative criteria well developed, expressed often through ridicule and a practical 'deconstructionist' eye for breaking down the 'reality effect'.

Katy: My husband likes the Carry On *films and oh, God, I mean, I've watched every one about three times, but he can watch them over and over again. When one comes on I always say 'You're not gonna watch this, I'm sick to death of them. You know exactly what's gonna happen next'. I like love stories (laughs). He'll watch them, but you know, he'll sit there taking the mickey.*

Lial: I have to watch it (Neighbours). *My girlfriend watches it and it's, ugh...I don't like soaps, they're boring. It's like they've got five houses and everything happens in those five houses. Abortions, people getting killed, dope, beating up, everything in those five houses! Not that much goes on around here! Too blown up and a waste of time!*

Despite this last quote, soap operas rather than programmed youth material were generally the most favoured TV forms in our discussion groups. TV ratings confirm this. Orders of preferences of all age groups, even down to primary school children, vary very little. Soaps provide materials with many possible interpretations and counter-identifications. They accept different readings and set up clear spaces for the symbolic work and active participation of different viewers. The realist orientation of evaluation amongst the young people we spoke to does not mean the more realism the better they like it. Rather there was a varying but intricate balance of taste quoted time and again between the appreciation of a realistic portrayal of a recognisable reality and an interest in glamour and the larger than life. The importance of programmes connecting in some way to life as it is actually lived emerges very strongly from the way young women talked about soap operas.

The soaps them more down to earth, I'm not being funny, but it's like the American soaps what are glamorous, 'cos I mean, look at Brookside... *Just normal people...But* Dallas *and all that, they seem to like to exaggerate everything, so lovely, and they're made of money. It's just something you watch to get out of life for a bit...But like* Eastenders *and* Brookside *you can't forget about the world.*

Although American soaps were enjoyed as a way to 'forget about your world for a bit' the immense popularity of the British shows rested on the way they explored problems and situations that young women could imagine themselves facing in a way that combined believability with drama and a dash of glamour. *Coronation Street* was sometimes disliked for getting this balance wrong.

Coronation Street, *I watch it, but I can't say that I really look forward to it, I mean, we always have it on, think it's routine, but I think it's a bit dreary really...I think it's just, I don't think anything exciting happens really in it. There isn't, you know...perhaps that's even more true to life. I think you want to get away from it a bit (laughs). It's mainly the pub, innit, I think nothing really happens in it and perhaps the people haven't got any glamour either.*

By the same token *Eastenders* was criticised for going overboard on drama.

They tried to smack everything in, like Michelle had the abortion, and Den knocking her off. You know what I mean, and they spoilt it really, they've got no story to it now, it's just boring. They've done all the story lines.

The variable relation between reality and representation and the very exaggeration of many soaps seemed to provide some important inputs towards a particular kind of informal symbolic work. This concerned the development of moral criteria for judging and assessing a range of real life situations which involve or might involve young people.

JC: What kinds of things are you learning (from the soaps)?
Sandra: Not to borrow money from the loan shark, 'cos Arthur was having a nervous breakdown and he started borrowing money and that.
Rachel: He's a fool.
Margaret: And not to mix with the wrong kind of people.
Sandra: Yeah, like drugs as well...Like Mary, she's a one...she's a single parent. But she's a prostitute, she's taking drugs now, which will be interesting to see. And Wixy, he's gonna catch AIDS the way he's carrying on.
Rachel: Why?
Sandra: ...he has a girl every single night, and I mean, he, he's just disgusting, he's so slack.
JC: Do you think that it's typical that a single mother that's on the dole becomes a -
Sandra: - If she's really desperate.
Rachel: It depends. She can be on the dole, have a child, but still live at home.
Margaret: Depends on how she's been brought up. If she had a lot of freedom.
Rachel: Because I know somebody who's a one parent family and she, she ain't nothin' like that, nothin' at all.
Sandra: It depends. If you ain't got no family or anything, and you live in a really bad flat, then they might decide to be

a prostitute. For that only purpose.

Altogether there is clearly a fine line between representation and reality. Reality itself depends on, and is in part constituted by representation - of images, arguments, moralities. But it is precisely the fine practical knowledge of this fine line which gives enjoyment - 'the pleasure of the text' - in the symbolic work and creativity of crossing and recrossing it, extending the fiction sometimes for yourself as well as deciding to take fiction as real for some purposes. An everyday aesthetic in viewing TV and in our discussion groups was precisely about this playfulness, not about realism as an absolute or as an expectation and assumption of 'truth' in images.

Margaret: ...then you want to see what happens next week, so you keep on carrying on watching it.
Sharma: That's it.
JC: Do you talk with your friends about these shows?
Several: Yeah.
Margaret: You watch it 'cos there's nothing else on the telly.
Rachel: When you watch the show, you don't really think like that. You just watch it for the enjoyment of it...you don't really think that people live like that.
Sharma: You like to predict it, don't you? Think of what's going to happen next.
Sandra: In Eastenders *I think some people are like that. Dirty Den...*
Yvonne: Sometimes it (Eastenders) *is boring. Yes, sometimes there isn't any story line. It's just like ordinary.*
Jo: The same, isn't it? Go to the pub for a drink, Pauline and Arthur!...Arthur's nicked some margarine from the store where he's been working and Pauline's going and the Gran's going um, um, um (laughs)...
Angela: That Gran gets on my nerves.
Jo: Michelle's frowning all the time. Moan, moan. She's a right mard that woman is. She's never happy.

From the external vantage point of many critics and commentators, soap operas are easily dismissed as wall-to-wall trivia, undemanding entertainment. But as our quotes show, the young women who watch them are constantly judging them and reworking the material they provide, finding echoes in their own lives and spaces which allow them to ask what would happen 'if'. TV watching is at least in part about helping the discussion about representation and reality as a general contribution to symbolic work and creativity. The audience is not an empty room waiting to be furnished in someone else's taste.

The fact that young people have an active, creative and symbolically productive relation to what they see on TV does not mean that what is provided has no 'effects'. But we need to find new ways of thinking about this familiar issue. Effects are the result, not of TV programmes, but of the creative relation of viewers with what they see. More and wider symbolic resources supplied through the TV screen would certainly enhance that relationship but not as a mechanical causation with measurable 'effects'. Instead of concentrating solely on the impact of particular programmes and of areas of content - such as violence - we should more properly consider what is missing or disappearing from the current schedules.

The widespread use of video tape recorders amongst the young should not be understood as a simple extension of TV-watching or cinema-going. It also has unique characteristics which change the nature of viewing in important ways. By releasing people from the pre-set schedules of the broadcasters and cinema managers it can make viewing a different kind of social experience as people gather in one another's houses to watch a new film or rock video release. It also gives viewers more control over the way they watch as well as over the materials of their own symbolic work. They can speed-scan the whole thing, skip sequences they don't like, repeat ones they do, slow the action down, and freeze a single frame on the screen. By allowing a more active relationship with the screen than is possible with conventional television viewing, these facilities open up new possibilities for everyday aesthetics in ways which begin to blur the line between consumption and production.

The latest addition to screen-based technologies is the micro-computer. Most young people use their micro-computers predominantly for games playing. From the vantage point of many adult observers this looks like a relatively trivial pursuit. But to many of those involved it is a richly creative and social activity which provides both an imaginative space and a basis for friendships and sociability.

Games involve a variety of skills ranging from hand eye co-ordination to bargaining, empathy and complex reasoning. In this situation people are no longer viewing a screen. They are interacting with it so that the progress or outcome of the scenario they are faced with depends mainly part on their actions. Active symbolic work is not just internal - it has external effects which in turn feed back further possibilities for symbolic work.

The more skilled users like Terry, an unemployed 21 year-old in Leicester, regularly write their own games.

Well, games are nice to play but I always have a go, I say 'I wonder if I could make that game' and then I try it myself.
Sometimes people come and say 'that's a nice programme,

did you buy it?' and I say, 'no I made it'. My talent seems to lie in making it look better...For a start, I look for a different presentation; the title screen etcetera, adding all little items like that...One of me greatest achievements was writing me own adventure programme where I could slot in any adventure I wanted. Certain problems would always occur, like you having to find a key to get through a door, or using a box to climb onto a shelf, that sort of problem. But also a maze which would calculate whether you could go through a wall with a magical potion or whatever. So you could move around and put little descriptions and everything into it.

Micro-computer users can also interact with other users or with a central data store, using a telecommunications link. Users can be linked in a vertical configuration with a central computer store of data and information. This has some interesting, but as yet largely unrealised, applications. For example, it could be used to allow young people to consult a community-based data store providing information of particular relevance to them using a terminal installed in public locations and accessible at a zero or nominal charge.

One way that 'vertical' communications networks are being used already however is for 'hacking', that is, making an unauthorised entry into a data base without paying the fee, or (in the case of governmental, military and corporate bases) without the necessary security clearance. The most spectacular recent instance is the case of 23 year-old Edward Austin Singh who used terminals at the University of Surrey to break into 250 protected data bases around the world. As with all hackers he used a pseudonym. He chose Sredni Vashtar, a ferret in a short story by Saki, but in a moment of high farce the University assumed they were dealing with a Russian spy.

Singh's level of expertise and ingenuity was unusual enough to put him among the 'hacking' elite. But in more modest forms the cracking of protection codes on commercial software or breaking into other kinds of protected data stores is not an unusual activity among young computer enthusiasts. One young Leicester man used his experience to win a bet with his father.

It's a programme that's very simple to make. It just keeps jiggling combinations. It's a system a lot have used to crack telephone numbers, 'cos this place is ex-directory, and me dad said 'you can't do it in a week' and I said 'yes I can'. And using the number plan and the telephone book and a bit of guess work as well I located the number. And he says 'I backed you twenty pounds that you can't do it in a week'. And I got my sister involved in it as well, and we ended up taking forty pounds off him. Served him right.

Usually there is no financial gain involved. The pleasure and grounded aesthetic is in solving the puzzle and beating the system. As another respondent explained,

I must admit I do have great fun trying to crack protection systems. But that's more to do with the fun of it, rather than anything to do with the programme once you've got it on tape.

Computers connected through the telecommunications system also allow users to communicate with each other without going through a central point. This is the principle behind the increasing number of bulletin boards and message systems, where users create electronic mail boxes and electronic magazines. Again, there is huge and yet unrealised potential here for extension and for young people's symbolic work and creativity.

Our fundamental point here is that the new screen-based technologies shouldn't be seen as simply extending television services. They have, or could have their own associated specific cultural practices. The new screen-based technologies are not widely available or used at the moment, but their potentials are immense.

Magazines such as *Jackie, Mizz* and *The Face* are very popular with young adult readers. They are liked not least because the reader 'can flip from beginning to end and over and over'. This might seem like young people opting for the easy read, for anything that isn't too much effort, drifting instead of working. But there is another form of symbolic work involved: the need to actually exercise the invited control over what and how much is read and with what degree of attention and with what links to outside events and experiences.

Magazines directly address young people, more so than newspapers. This, combined with the fact that the young person has probably actually bought the magazine, makes it a possession symbolically important in the creation of a self- identity. Magazines are carefully kept after reading, even if never re-read.

Young women and increasingly young men develop their external image in part by using magazine hints on fashion and appearance.

Angela: Mizz, *that's a good book for fashion.* Smash Hits *and things like that. You just see clothes and you think, I like that...*

Jo: I get Vogue, Just Seventeen... *Well, it's my sister who gets it, so I have a look at it, you know, and* Over 21 *for all the fashion...*

JC: Tell me about Mizz.

Angela: Well, it has people wearing clothes that haven't

*come in, like, you know, and then you start seeing people
wearing them.*

These young women, and others, report that they also get their
fashion ideas from looking carefully at people on the streets, at how
their friends dress and at television shows like *The Clothes Show.*
Keeping up with the ever-changing world of fashion is difficult for these
young women given their limited resources. Doing so is of utmost
importance to them. Figuring out how to dress their bodies requires
that they learn a subtle symbolic system, and then decide which of its
components fit with and express their identity. But in establishing their
identity they also walk the tightrope between an individual sense of
themselves, and a construction which obeys the rules of what a
woman is meant to look like. Many young women respond to fashion
images at the same time being critical of magazine imagery: 'They
pressurise you to be attractive/beautiful etc like models'; 'I become
increasingly depressed seeing sylph like women when I'm on the
plump side!'.

The advice columns in magazines tend to be much read and
provide young women with knowledge and understanding about their
personal and family lives. They can also be much criticised and
parodied.

*Hilary: The problem pages! 'Dear Aunt Clara, I fancy this
boy in my class and he don't fancy me. I've asked him out
and he's told me to fuck off. Please will you help me'.
JC: What's the advice?
Hilary: Find someone else, love, don't worry about him.
Yvonne: They just say, let this boy make his move when he
wants and make yourself look nice for him, and he'll make
his move if he really fancies you. If not, forget him.*

Young women at one and the same time recognise the 'genre' of
problem pages, and send them up - as in Yvonne's case - dismissing
the traditional view of relationships in which girls are simply passive
bystanders.

Young women can also be highly critical of 'soppy' love stories and
their limitations, whilst somehow enjoying their very familiarity.

*Hilary: These are the kind of stories that the magazines
have, 'Sarah was 16, and her packed Andy in for Steve, but
she found out that Steve loved her more than whatever his
name was and he was knocking off someone else. What
could she do, she used to cry at night'. At the end they get
back together and that's the end of the story. And that's all
that ever happens.*

The fact that Hilary dismisses the happy ending, suggests that she uses the symbols with which romantic love is constructed in a different way to that proposed, one which takes into account a more complex and realistic understanding of relationships.

Young women, and some young men, use articles about pop stars as a resource they can work on further, as Katy, Rachel and Jo explain.

JC: Is there stuff about music or stars?

Rachel: Stars, fact files. Like one person out of a group, and it gives you your (sic) name, birthdate, interest, hobbies, married, dislikes, favourite food, music, cars...Like it tells you how they made their video.

Jo: They write the song out and it's there for you. So when it's on you can sing along (laughs) in your bedroom. I learn all the words from it.

JC: Do you ever cut things out of magazines and put them on the walls? What kind of things do you cut out?

Jo: Posters. Pop stars.

JC: Do you ever make posters with little things from them?

Katy: I done this facts cover about George Michael, 'cos I'm crazy on him. I got all the fact files and music, song words and all that.

JC: Do you put that on them all or cut it out?

Katy: I just like made a book into it, like. Scrap book...

Young women use their preferences for one star over another to help decide the criteria they consider important in relationships and to see how they differ from their peers in their taste in men. Pop stars are, to some extent, symbolic vehicles with which young women understand themselves more fully, even if by doing so they may partly shape their personalities to fit the stars' alleged preferences. At the same time, in developing a relationship with the male pin-up decorating her bedroom wall, she is doing what the male does - imagining, in a controlled way, how to place this man in her life.

These activities often occur in 'bedroom culture'(4) the most private space in which young women act and interact with each other. The bedroom is a place where young women talk among themselves and try to understand their relationships with parents, siblings and boyfriends. More significantly, in doing so they are learning to articulate the emotional criteria with which their inner selves are constituted. They learn, that is, about their own and other peoples' motives by closely scrutinising all the relationships in which they are involved.

6 Style and Fashion

Clothes, style and fashion have long been recognised as key elements in young people's expression, exploration and the making of their individual and collective identities. They remain amongst the most visible forms of symbolic cultural creativity and informal artistry in people's lives. As in other areas we have looked at, everyday aesthetics are at play even in apparently passive consumption. Creative consumption stretches into and lies on a continuum with more obviously creative activities.

Clothes shopping has been a central part of post-war youth cultural consumerism. As a cultural practice, however, shopping has tended to be marginalised in much of the writing about youth, style and fashion: it has been considered a private and feminine activity and part of the process of incorporation into the social machinery.

But young people don't just buy passively or uncritically. They transform, appropriate and recontextualise. Young consumers break the ordered categories, the suggested matches and ideas promoted by shops. They bring their own specific grounded aesthetics to bear on consumption, choosing their own colours and matches and personalising their purchases. Many young people combine elements of clothing to create new meanings. They adopt and adapt clothing items drawn from government surplus stores, for example, or from sportswear shops.

While many of the young people we spoke to obtain their ideas about clothes from friends or from simply observing how clothes look worn on other people, many also use the media to understand and keep up with the latest fashions. They get ideas about clothes from television programmes, like *The Clothes Show*, fashion and music magazines and from the personal dress styles of particular pop artists. Aspects of the clothes and outfits worn by pop groups like Bananarama and Amazulu, for example, were taken up en masse by young women in the early and mid-80s, particularly haystack hairstyles, dungarees and children's plimsolls.

There is now a long and well-known list of youth subcultural styles, from the teddy-boys and the mods to the skins and punks which have occupied the attention of sociologists, journalists and fashion commentators alike. The distinct styles of post-war youth subcultures have been interpreted as symbolic solutions to age and class domination, and a means of marking out and winning 'cultural space' for young people. Such styles have been lauded for their symbolic work in borrowing and transforming everyday objects or fashion components. Examples include the teds' appropriation of the Edwardian suit, the skins' appropriation of proletarian work clothes, or the punks' borrowing of safety pins, bin liners and zips.

While only a small minority of young people adopted the complete uniform of youth subcultures, large numbers drew on selective elements of their styles creating their own meanings and uses from them. Many subcultural styles became popularised, finding their way into mainstream working class and middle class youth culture. In this way, subcultures became a source of inspiration for all young people. Punk, for example, stimulated a move back to straight legged trousers, smaller collars and shorter hair amongst young people of all ages. The leggings/thermal underpants first worn by punk girls - which were originally cream and had to be dyed black - were soon being made up new by young market-stall holders. By the summer of 1985 they were being produced in T-shirt cotton and a wide range of colours and had become a definitive fashion item for all women under the age of 40.

Since and including the punk explosion, one of the most important trends in youth style has been the rehabilitation and raiding of previous sartorial styles for raw material in young people's symbolic work and creativity, stylistic and cultural expression. 'Retro' style is part of a trend in contemporary culture which ransacks various historical moments for their key stylistic expressions and then recombines and re-inserts them in current fashion. Clothing items are worn as though in quotation marks, their wearers self-consciously evoking some past event at the risk of stylistic mismatch and incongruity. These references to past stylistic forms have taken on a kind of iconographic status in pop culture, evoking periods of social history, and have been used extensively in popular music and advertising.

Clothes, like musical tastes, indicate leisure orientations of different groups of young people. Young people are adept at the symbolic work of developing their own styles and also at 'reading off' and decoding the dress styles of others and relating them to musical, political and social orientations. Thus, as one young woman noted, people who liked 'house music' dressed in the 'house style' - Doc Martens shoes/ boots, scarves, baggy shirts, old checked jackets with long collars, baggy trousers, 'things that don't fit you, but look smart'.

But clothes signify more than just musical tastes. No longer are they an automatic reflection of subcultural affiliations or collective social identities. Clothes are also an important medium for everyday aesthetics in which young people express and explore their own specific individual identities. Young people learn about their inner selves partly by developing their outer image through clothes. They use style in their symbolic work to express and develop their understanding of themselves as unique persons, to signify who they are, and who they think they are. As one young woman put it, 'If I find something I know I like, if I know I like certain clothes then I know I'm that kind of person'.

Young people's uses and choices of clothes also involve a process of conscious, purposeful image-making. Clothes can be used playfully for the sheer pleasure of putting together a costume, or fabricating an identity. As one young woman said,

> To me, what you wear in a morning and what you wear to go out is a fancy dress, that's all I see it as because you enjoy the clothes you wear, right?...To me, fancy dress is everyday clothes, what you wear to college, go out to work or whatever, or what you wear to go out, it is fancy dress costume...I mean, you've got a costume on now, haven't you? I've got a costume on, everybody's got a costume on...

Young people make clear distinctions between everyday clothes for college or work, and clothes for going out. They are used symbolically to mark the boundaries between leisure and work. Dressing to go out at night or at the weekend is an important activity which involves symbolic work and specific pleasures all of its own. Clothes are absolutely central in courtship rituals amongst young people. They are used not only to attract the opposite sex, but also to gain friends, win peer group acceptance, and to appear different or interesting. Young people frequently 'put on' identities when they go out, a process which includes not only dressing-up but also role-playing and putting on different accents. Joan, for example, reports that she wants to look 'different' and to have people think that she is different when she goes out. She wanted to show a different side of her personality from that in college, which involved her talking and dressing differently.

> You don't want to look the same all the time, do you, you want to look totally different when you go out at night...When I go out, they don't recognise me, because I am totally dressed up, and they think that isn't Joan, when they look at you good and proper, they think, 'God, you look totally different', and that's what you want, you don't want to look the same when you go out.

The grooming, cutting and styling of hair is an important cultural practice and symbolic activity for all young people. Hair has long been a medium of significant 'statements' about self and society in which symbolic meanings are invested. Hairstyle has also been a central component in a variety of subcultural expressions: from the DA quiff of the teds to the long hair of the hippies to the crop of the skinheads.

Hairstyling practices amongst black British youth are a particularly lively and creative field where young people are able to seize some degree of symbolic control in their everyday lives. Black hairstyles are popular art forms which articulate a variety of aesthetic solutions to the problems created by racism. For hair, along with skin-colour, is one of the most visible signs of racial difference. Racism, historically, has devalued the material qualities of black people's hair, seeing it only in negative terms. Aesthetics which stem from Western codes of beauty where whiteness epitomises all that is good, true and beautiful have long been used to rationalise racial domination.

In the 60s black liberation movements proposed the slogan 'Black is Beautiful' to contest the hegemony of this white 'aesthetics' with a grounded aesthetics of its own. Fully aware that such hegemony depended on the subjective internalisation of these norms and values, the Afro hairstyle was adopted by Afro-Americans as an outward affirmation of an empowering sense of Black Pride. In the Caribbean context, the popularisation of Rastafarian beliefs served a similar purpose. Dreadlocks became emblematic of a newly discovered sense of self. After centuries of negation, such styles inverted the binary logic of white bias to celebrate the natural qualities of black hair.

Hair has thus been a key area of semantic struggle over the significance of racial difference, a struggle to negate the very categories of racial oppression itself. In Rastafari, for example, the open signification of dreadness, through the growing of locks, transposes the difference already immanent in the acceptable attribute of dark skin into open symbolic struggle, drawing attention to that least acceptable attribute of 'blackness' - woolly hair.

In the 1980s, however, these forms of cultural resistance drawing on a grounded aesthetic of naturalness and authenticity have been joined by another set of cultural strategies in the medium of hair. These turn around an everyday aesthetic of artifice that works in and against the codes of the dominant culture, through deliberate mixing and the unusual combination of different styles. Innovation occurs through appropriations of elements from the dominant culture marked off and differentiated by a creolising logic of re-accentuation.

In accordance with these strategies the 80s has seen a striking diversity in hairstyles amongst black British youth, in tune with constantly evolving and more fluid forms of black British culture. The 80s has seen a revival of processed black American hairstyles from the 40s and 50s (such as the conk and the Do Rag) as well as contemporary styles like curly perms (hair treated by steaming, relaxing and straightening) and flat tops.

Traditionally read as a sign of self-oppression or aspiring to white ideals, straightening and processed hairstyling techniques are increasingly seen as providing the materials for an open symbolic creativity rather than as inert signs of an 'inner' self-image, or be read as a sign of alienation or in-authenticity. Straightening is merely one technique among others, and a means to a symbolic end. As one young woman pointed out,

Just because you do your hair in a particular way doesn't alter your attitude as a black person - or it shouldn't anyway.

What constitutes blackness is itself subject to historical change and negotiation. As one young black man put it,

The way we conceptualise Africa, is based on myth, textual references. You know a lot of Caribbeans have not been to Africa.

There is no such thing as total originality. Sources of style are always already culturally formed, already in play. Nothing is totally new. Young black people may choose and shift between many different available hairstyles, drawing on diverse roots for symbolic resources and stylistic inspiration such as books, magazines and museums as well as particular black stars in music, fashion, film or sport. Thus people make reference to Grace Jones haircuts (flat top), or Egyptian style shapes to a haircut. Such references are informed by an awareness of black hair styles in a historical tradition, a tradition in which young black people consciously position themselves.

The everyday aesthetics of black hairstyling have their own terms and criteria of evaluation. Choosing what kind of style and cut involves important decisions, beginning from whether or not to cut one's hair. Dreadlocks for example are based on not cutting and involve long-term cycles of growth and cultivation. Cutting and the decisions which follow on involve choosing from a range of techniques and styles.

7 Drinking and Fighting

We've chosen to end our sample of fieldwork on a difficult and controversial note - is it possible to find threads of meaning, even grounded aesthetics, in a presentation of the most profane and contemptible of common everyday activities: drinking and fighting. We do this partly out of a sense of completeness. These things certainly involve large sections of youth, especially the white male working class. While we certainly do not wish to fan the flames of sensation we also feel that it is quite wrong to avert our gaze selectively and conveniently when trouble looms, and to miss out tracts of the social and symbolic landscape which actually constitute the terrain underfoot as well as, often, the effective horizon for many young people.

This does not mean that we applaud or support such activities. Apart from their intrinsic destructiveness, they also help to reproduce oppressive race, class and gender structures of feeling, attitude and practice. Male violence must always be referenced to the omnipresence of a heterosexual, white, male hegemony. Nevertheless, more than one thing can be true of, or said about, a phenomenon. Another reason for including the following material is that it constitutes a kind of 'limit case' for the argument. If we can find a thread of symbolic work and coherent human meaning and feeling even in brutalised conditions and through degrading materials, then our general argument is demonstrated all the more effectively. This thread of meaning could swell into streams and rivers through sympathetic materials and welcoming symbolic channels.

In part our purpose here is to get behind the tabloid headlines to get at real human contexts and meanings. It is ironic that the physical fight on stage or the celluloid image is accepted as a legitimate climax to other kinds of symbolic fighting. It is taken as an understandable resolution to a tense chain of events connected through the meanings of plot and situation. Yet our images and understandings of urban violence in real life are ridiculously truncated. We're transfixed by the notion, symbolically, of 'gratuitousness'. Fights are cut off from prior and surrounding symbolic meanings: from all that went before, from the narratives, contexts and meanings which place and make them - these things which for the participants often remove precisely their 'gratuity'.

To reverse the currently fashionable banalities about screen violence leading to real violence, it is certainly possible to suggest that something of our very capacity to accept and interpret violence in dramatic contexts may well (invisibly) depend on our own knowledge of the informal dynamics of aggression. This includes understanding the difficulty of seeking appeasement with dignity, appreciating the seemingly irrevocable cast of some events, and accepting that there are moments when no words will do but actions speak loud. Violence can have a symbolic as well as a physical part to play in social interaction.

Drinking in pubs is an important leisure activity, especially for white young men. Three quarters of the 16-24 age group visit pubs, on average, nearly four times a week (5). It is much less common for Afro-Caribbeans and for most young Asians. Young people go to pubs for many reasons. One important reason is simply to escape boredom and the restrictions of the parental home. As Steve says,

If you stop in the house with your family, I just moan. I wish I was going out. Even if you go and tidy your room up, they have a go at you...So you've got to go out somewhere. I think if I had to stop in the house, they start getting on my nerves and I start getting on their nerves, after a while, like. You know, they have nothing to do so they start getting on to you...When you're in the house like...it's the same four walls all the time. So it's great to see somebody different, even if you're just sitting in the pub, you're looking at something.

If you are looking for somewhere to go, it's hardly surprising that it should be the pub. It is one of the most, if not *the,* central leisure institutions of white adult British culture. Young people turn towards it not only for 'something to do' but also as a way of identifying *with* adults, of becoming more adult and seeking acceptance *by* adults as *an adult.* The under-age thrill of successfully ordering alcohol in public, in 'The Public', is one of the markers of passing from childhood.

The pub is also a social environment which announces immediately that here is a place which is about relaxation, leisure and pleasure - polar opposites to the formal qualities of work and school. The direct effect of alcohol relaxes the self and distances the real world as does the warmth, size, comfort and protection of the pub. But the 'good pub' is one that concentrates many good things, as one young man said, 'Women, cheap beer, good beer, loud music'. The media shape young people's leisure activities throughout and the pub is no exception. Pubs are enjoyable partly because they allow young people to see and hear videos of the latest pop hits as well as classic 'evergreens'. They also allow access to expensive media and playback hardware beyond the reach of domestic finances.

Steve: There's one (a satellite dish to receive MTV, the music video television station) in a pub in Bilston, Bull's Head. You used to have to pay for a video in there, 50p for two sides. Now you just sit there and watch MTV...The in-thing is CDs, compact discs. You pay 50p for two sides on the CD. The thing is, it's off albums, not just the chart thing.

Neil: You get maybe on a juke box a hundred songs. On a compact disc you get 2,000. 'Cos them only small. They'm excellent. On a juke box like, it's singles. You know, the 45s, but on a compact disc; it's the album and you can have what track you want off each album like...

From the point of view of space, architecture, design, technology and devotion to pleasure, pubs are much grander than the home. That is obviously part of their attraction. But this is not the end of the story. There are more illicit pleasures. For many young men, the entry into the pub, especially on a Saturday night, is also the start or the promise of a kind of adventure - reflected symbolically in some of the more outlandish 'theme styling' of refurbished 'leisure pubs'. This adventure or promise is about the suspension of the given, the mundane and the everyday. It starts in the head and in the immediate social group with the physical effects of alcohol, but it produces changes whose ripples can and do spread to make waves outside.

The social context of drinking operates to maximise consumption for many young men. There's no shame in it. It's done with others. Round-buying reflects and reinforces social and cultural solidarity. It is often a competitive activity. The amount consumed is related to how much of a 'man' you are, and the 'men' encourage each other in their 'manliness'.

Dean: When you're drinking, you always want to drink more than the other person. You always think you can take the most. If you go drinking, you're a man.

For young women, by contrast and to underline the case, drinking is not social, nor competitive, nor encouraged by the group. Excess consumption certainly emphases public gender identity but in ways which are felt to be negative - especially given the realities of dealing with a predatory and sexist environment.

Sandra: It's not feminine (to drink in excess). My friend, she got drunk and I just left her there and then. 'Cos she was just slaggin' around. And I just, I just said, 'If you're gonna be like that, that's your problem'. And I just walked out. And

I went home.

Being drunk produces uncertainty and with it, potential danger. In particular, however unjustly and unfairly, it runs the risk of being perceived to be 'slaggin' around' - immoderately displaying sexual availability.

For young men, however, there seems to be a welcoming of uncertainty and its possible dangers. It defeats boredom and seems to open up symbolic and real possibilities not available in normal life. They view drinking as that which sets up a situation, an atmosphere, where anything might happen. The physiological effects of alcohol are interpreted to mean loss of control - an existential freeing of the self to an uncertainty which seems to be 'new' or 'different' every time. It opens the way to adventure whose possibility constitutes a kind of grounded aesthetics of risk, risk-taking and lack of (routine) determinacy. Risk is esteemed. The unexpected adventures which follow might be trivial: a bet, a 'piss-take', cheeking others or elders. They might be nothing at all except a frisson or heightened atmosphere of possibility with your mates in the pub. They might be serious, or escalate into it: setting out to gatecrash a party; being stopped by the police; getting into a fight; passing out in strange places. It's almost as if some young men want to invent through drink their own trials by performance in uncertain situations. The kinds of risks they take, the way they structure these risks, the way they deal with them, indicate, of course, components of young masculinity. Such components include improvisation, 'wit', 'guts', indifference to pain resulting from foolhardy actions, devil-may-care irresponsibility.

David: When you've had a bit of drink, you'd do
anything...you just feel wild more than anything.
Dean: You feel lucky as well.
David: No matter how big they am, you think, I'll have a go
at him.
Andrew: Sometimes you go drinking and you go home,
pissed out of your brains, and the next day you think, 'Was it
reality or a dream?'.
David: Sometime ago me mom found me in the verandah,
just lying flat. I must have passed out.
Dean: I've jumped in the canal pissed and everything, off the
bridge. You do all sorts of funny things, don't you?
Andrew: You find it ever so funny when you do it. I mean, if
somebody fell over, you'd laugh your head off.
Dean: You wouldn't be able to stop laughing. Or someone
would say, 'Go and do this'. And you'll go and do it.
Andrew: You do mad things that you wouldn't dare.

The sense of release, adventure and possibility is partly about the symbolic creativity of overthrowing, ignoring or transcending conventions and normally approved patterns of behaviour and activity. These are seen often as, by definition, restrictive and boring. Many young people feel that they have no possibilities for 'safe adventures'. This may say as much about the conventional possibilities we provide as about the risky and anti-social ones they pursue.

Drinking is often associated with fighting, but in many ways they have contrary dynamics - though they can enravel with disastrous consequences.

The fundamental issue for most young men in urban areas and locations where there hangs a fear of violence is not to fight as often as possible, but as little as possible. Most of all, the aim is to maintain honour and reputation whilst escaping intimidation and 'being picked on'. To achieve this you have to grapple with the complexities of 'hardness' in social performance.

Jonathan: It's a sort of feeling of being known as a hard person. Like sort of going around and knowing that no one's gonna mess with you because you'm hard...Being hard is all to do with how you put yourself across.

'Hardness' can be both an inner and an outer quality. It is also related directly to masculinity, its codes and public honours. There are several permutations of hardness with performance. All have their relation to masculine reputation.

Jonathan: How hard you act and how hard you am are two different things. Like there's some people who act really hard but they just ain't at all. Put down in one punch.
Whereas other people keep themselves to themselves and you go up to them, you have a fight with them, and they take your punch, no trouble, and when they throw a punch at you, you know about it.
Andrew: You can be hard and act hard, and you can not act hard and be hard, or you can act hard and not be hard. I think the best of them is to be hard and not act hard...

The space between inner and outer meanings is worked through in what can be thought of quite literally as a dramatic grounded aesthetic: acting out your own performance and interpreting the public performances of others.

Steve: You got to watch people like, and see how they'm acting. You can always tell when they'm trying to act as if they'm hard, you can always tell the quiet ones. They just stand there...The quiet ones nearly always turn out to be the hardest.

The worst of the permutations is to be somebody who acts hard but is not really hard 'inside'. Such a person creates an external persona that is unmatched by bodily force and skill. He is not what he appears to be. He is in danger because of this.

Steve: If you keep yourself to yourself, nothing will happen, but if you start going around acting hard or something, when you ain't, people are going to come down on you.

Someone who acts and is hard is preferable. At least the exterior is matched by inner qualities. But the most respected permutation is dissimulation, 'to be hard and not act hard'. This is to have substance, the 'right stuff', but not feel the need to display it.

Neil: A mate'll respect you if you walk away from drunkenness.

Steve: If anyone comes up to you and says 'Do you want a fight?', you say, 'Fuck off'. If they don't, you just beat them up. You give them a chance to walk away. Say, 'I don't want to fight, alright? I don't want no trouble, just go away like'. You'm still standing your ground, you'm standing there saying, 'go away'.

The one who is provoked speaks before hitting. Respect is gained by negotiating with an antagonist. This is part of 'standing your ground' and is preferable to fighting. None of this works, however, unless you are prepared to fight *in extremis*. The shadow and the substance intertwine. The performance and the inner reality overlap.

There is a tight moral and dramatic economy here. But it can easily break down. External appearances are not a good guide to the reality of danger. It is not easy to judge the line where giving someone the chance to walk away becomes undignified appeasement. It is not easy to maintain both dignity and safety. Symbolic rather than physical management of tension is always preferred by most, and provides the norms for behaviour. But real fighting remains the final arbitration. 'Hard-knocks' and 'nut-cases' who seem to like fighting and who can offer unexpected open and demeaning provocation have to be dealt with. For some reason they don't know, or won't play, 'the game'.

More importantly, drink routinely complicates or de-stabilises the balance of the dramatic economy. Its buzz, frisson and grounded aesthetics of risk enable the unexpected; 'one thing leads to another', somebody feels 'lucky' or 'wild' so 'anything can happen'. Drink makes unreasonable attack and foolhardy defence much more likely. Were it not for 'hard-knocks' and drink, the menacing aspects of urban social life might simply resolve into a series of honourable stand-offs. But when the gauntlet is thrown down, masculine honour seems to demand an answer. Aided by drink, the drama becomes compulsive.

Andrew recounted the events surrounding a fight he'd been involved in recently. He and his mate were drunk, his mate had been beaten up, and those around him were then calling him a 'wanker' for not fighting single-handedly against the large group that had beaten up his mate.

Andrew: Everyone was calling me a wanker...In a way I felt I had to do it (fight) to prove myself I was strong...To prove I weren't scared of them. I mean, I was (scared)...I mean, I wouldn't do it if I was sober. I wouldn't go, 'Oh, fuck, lets go and get battered by twenty kids!' I'll just look harder...and they won't call me a wanker...When you'm pissed, you go fuck, you can have your head split.

Andrew had to fight not just to defend his mate but, more importantly, his own honour and standing. Harsh, it seems unanswerable, judgements and exclusions wait on failure.

Andrew: They'd just laugh and leave you out. Say, forget about you. 'He didn't hit back, so we may as well forget him now.'

Sometimes it's necessary to lose physically in order to win psychologically and socially. Once embarked however unwillingly on a violent encounter there seems to arise another darker excitement that eclipses some of the previous moral and social calculus. This is the incomprehensible buzz of the momentary disappearance of all meaning allied to almost superhuman feelings of omnipotence and power. Courting this prospect may lead a minority to deliberately provoke incidents - 'nutters' and 'hard-knocks' certainly, but also sometimes 'normal' kids who are drunk, bored 'out of their minds', 'pissed off' about something, or desperate to find energy and excitement from somewhere *that night*.

Those who've been involved in fights say that they feel suddenly stronger, experience no pain, and find the situation strangely compelling.

Andrew: I've found that when I'm drunk, I'm stronger...When you'm drunk as well, you don't feel the pain...You feel the force, but not the pain. It's a weird sensation, scary and good. People like to be scared, like on roller coasters...scary because it's different, you ain't used to it. That's why it's scary. But it's good 'cos you ain't feeling it. You can go back for longer.

This feeling of reckless strength is essential to any real prospect of winning a fight. It is part of, tests and reproduces 'hardness' - being able to detonate an explosion of physicality in extreme situations. Andrew again,

It's just a waste of time having a fight if you don't feel hard.
Then you know you'm gonna lose, aren't you? I mean, you
got to feel hard to think you've got a chance to win. You
have to feel confidence.

Crucial to displacing finer feelings and fear with a robotic brutality
is the notion of losing your temper. David and Andrew say that they
feel no pain in a fight because they 'get in a temper'. Losing your
temper seems to be losing yourself as well, losing the hum-drum of the
everyday, momentarily, for an entirely different state of being.

Keith: You don't feeling nothing. When they'm hitting you,
you don't know.

Andrew: You'm so busy concentrating...You feel the hit, but
you don't feel the pain. Pressure, but no pain.

David: You'd just want to hit him and concentrate on hitting
him. If someone just punched you without (you) being in a
temper, it would hurt. If it was unexpected. But once you'm
in a temper, you just don't care. You don't give a toss.

JC: Is it exciting, then, when you're in a temper?...You don't
feel anything?

Andrew: It's excitement, really isn't it?

Keith: Then it's all over, isn't it! (laughs) It's over too quick.
You don't realise what's happened and then when you walk
away, you say, 'Did I win? Or did I lose? Or what!'.

Being in a fight seems to heighten your sense of reality by
removing you from its conventions. The usual capacity to see events
unfold is lost; there is no past, no future, only a very consuming
present. This radical transformation of reality is exciting, yet ephemeral,
gone as soon as it is experienced. Such intense and consuming
absorption in the present makes it difficult to develop a narrative
sequence to explain and place events, 'Who won, who lost, or what?'.

There's an interesting connection to the media violence debate
here. For these young men, it is not that violent media images
fascinate because they lead to copycatting, it's more that their own
lives provide the raw experience. The media images can help to shape
and give this experience a grammar, a language and a representation.
Media images fascinate because they can be used to name and to
make comparisons. They can be used as symbolic material to make
sense of that incoherent but exciting experience which in the heat of
the conflict seems to be without its own meaningful signs and
symbols. Media images can be used to try to make sense of how
something can be exciting and incredibly scary at the same time,
controlled from outside and numbing but also exhilarating - 'like a roller
coaster'. TV images are used to try to convey the terrible fascination

and as a way of trying, impossibly, to give a narrative to the incomprehensible.

David: It's like you'm watching it and it's coming at you, but you can't feel it.

Keith: It's like the telly, you can't feel the punches, but you'm giving them out like.

David: It's like someone's punching on the TV screen at you and you can't feel it.

JC: How's that like the telly?

Keith: 'Cos you watch it and you don't get hurt.

Andrew: You could give me shit and beat me with anything, sticks, the lot, and it's horrible, it, like, you aren't there, as though you'm watching. It's like you see on the telly, it's scary, really. That's the scary part.

Keith: You could of got killed then and wouldn't have known about it.

Andrew: It ain't getting beat up that's scary, it's that you can't feel anything and you don't know what's happening.

Later from another discussion.

Keith: They bust your nose, didn't they?

Andrew: Yeah, bust me nose up.

Keith: Right across your face, it was, wasn't it? Like Rocky.

It must now be recognised that violence is irredeemably part of our modern culture. For some young men fighting unleashes a seemingly uncontrolled and uncontrollable power. This power is admired and exciting yet simultaneously dangerous and frightening. Both emotions are way beyond the range of middle class and conventional notions of the importance of control at all times, except perhaps in the safe outer reaches of 'Art for Arts Sake'. 'Hardness' has very wide currency and respect. It indicates the readiness, if necessary and under pressure, to risk the self to, and try to control, the dangerous and contradictory forces of violence.

Ironically, the cultural system which limits and places this dangerous power is very much about control and performance: a *drama* of presenting and reading appearance and intention. To be lacking in control is very much looked down on. Control and power, very real physical and social stakes and the inherent risks and meanings of being outside the law, make violence and its associated dramas potent symbolic materials to displace or disrupt given official and institutional meanings. These materials help in the construction and reconstruction of alternative ways of being in and seeing the world, of alternative values and ways of valuing people.

Some of these values may be repellent. They undoubtedly help to reproduce a certain kind of masculinity, as well as reproducing a dangerous acceptance of unacceptable violence. This has particular implications for women in the home where symbolic disputes can all too easily find a physical resolution. It can spill over as a threatening quality into the whole of our common cultural experience making public space unsafe for all, but especially for women and for other target groups ('pakis', 'poofs') for an aggressive masculinity. But these values and identities also concern a desperate kind of honour, a strange respect for the space around dignity and a mad courage which confronts banality with really live drama. Whether we like them or not, these are some of the contradictory living arts of survival - physical, psychic, cultural. Horrifyingly, hynotisingly, they contain some of their own specific grounded aesthetics. Outside condemnation, without understanding or suggestion of alternative, show up the limits of the observer as well as those of the observed. Alternatives to, ideas and plans for the safer resolutions of, the compelling dramas of violence should be what exercise our imaginations.

8 Implications

Policy statements and documents concerned with the arts or culture may speak volumes, but too often do no more than speak on shelves. The problem with most attempts at formulating cultural policy is that they tend to reflect the choices of small and unrepresentative groups of people and often reject, as a matter of course, all the choices that have been made by the majority of people with whom they happen to disagree. The difficulty we face in deriving policy statements from this report is how not to emulate this tradition.

We do not, therefore, in conclusion to the report, suggest fine line blue-prints for cultural policy. We aim rather to shift the terms of debate and open up new areas - not just narrowly for 'Arts Policy' but for all policies which affect young people.

The point we want to emphasise is that we are all cultural producers in some way and of some kind in our everyday lives. Especially so are young people. That which the 'arts establishment' has been attempting to encourage *is already there* - though the terms, accents and articulations are different. The real arts now, their symbolic materials and resources and the manner of their use, are different from those of the nineteenth century which still dominate our thinking. They are different perhaps not so much in their contents, aesthetics, as in all their relations - their institutions, manner of supply, consumption and production, their connections to commerce and to social structure. We should not criticise or bemoan these new relations but try to understand them and their convergence with youth's own attempt at making modern identities, at culture-making.

In particular it has to be understood that we are now living in a thoroughly artefactable, commodified and mediated culture. We need new concepts for art *in*, not co-existent with, the age of commodity and media culture. Formerly it was usually a live *human performance* which was the focus of attention, at the centre of culture, with artefacts, texts or scores, in the background as guides. Now culture has many centres, and most often the text *and* performance are unified in single artefacts which are then commodified as pop songs, videos, films and distributed to widely disparate 'audiences' through the cultural media. Performance has disappeared from the centre. The organic process of preparing for, and playing to, an audience has been transformed and de-centred. Often the whole 'live' process is now organised *backwards* from the point of view of achieving the best possible final commodity form, rather than *forwards* as the simple recording of what the audience would have been given anyway. Artefacts as commodities are taken up into a wholly new mediation with much wider 'audiences' in some of the ways our fieldwork has presented. We need to understand the new creative, communal processes on the other side of commodified artefacts and on the other side of their mass distribution, processes not of performance, but, if you like, the *performances* of creative consumption in ordinary, common culture.

In fact, cultural commodities are often not consumed at all. They take part in many 'performances'. They don't cease to exist once used. Compact discs, for instance, can be used over and over again without any wear or deterioration. The same musical item can be 'consumed' repeatedly in widely heterogeneous ways and in very different contexts. All these uses bring with them their own associated possibilities of cultural significance and of their own grounded aesthetics.

Perhaps we should see the real locus of creativity and variety not in orginal performances at all, but in the multi-form 'consumptions' of common culture. Mass cultural pessimism should yield to mass creativity optimism. The fixation on unitary forms, contents and performances and on their internal aesthetics is a nineteenth century construct and constricts if not strangles the modern possibilities of common culture. We need twenty first century ways of understanding cultural *processes* very different from static, minority and elite notions of 'culture' as the making, performance or appreciation of special or unique, artistic *things*.

These new cultural processes are simply not recognised in public debate, still less in policy and practice. Subsidy is still directed, for instance, at making live performance seats cheaper for a minority of the usually already well-off. It might be directed at making cultural commodities (recordings, videos, reproduction equipment) cheaper for the repeated, creative consumptions of youth and other low-income groups whose relative poverty often bars or limits access to the necessary and elementary resources of common culture.

We have attempted throughout the report to recognise and represent the practices and processes of everyday cultural life, to understand creative work undertaken there with the available symbolic materials - what we call a grounded or everyday aesthetic i.e. an aesthetic grounded in the needs and functions of everyday life. The policy imperative should be to enhance this creativity in all ways possible, from convential means to experimental ones. This is not a narrow question of adding something extra, or of bringing to informal cultures things quite unlike themselves. Cultural policy questions concern the recognition of practices which are already there - encouraging them and opening to their cultural production the widest possible range of symbolic resources and materials through which people can symbolically express their intentions, attitudes and hopes.

Such imperatives of everyday aesthetics involve issues and institutions of a much wider range than have hitherto been encompassed within the 'cultural' realm and lead us into many policy areas and processes not so far designated as 'cultural'. The point of intervention should be, by awareness and deliberate policy, to tilt more of these processes more to the advantage of young people. Everyday aesthetics are essential to the ways in which young people make sense of the social world and their place within it, allowing them to see beyond the immediate requirements and contradictions of work, family and the dole. It is this widest symbolic creativity which should be recognised and promoted in the provision of the general conditions and spaces that can allow young people's cultural practices to flourish - to create the supportive environmental, economic and social conditions which enable them to do better and more creatively what they do already.

In relation to this 'doing already', a very important theme of the report has been the complex and varied role of cultural commodities and the modern cultural media in the symbolic work and creativity of young people. As we have seen, simple mechanistic notions of mass marketing and mass production enforcing their own debased forms of mass consumption are simply not helpful here. The cultural world is much more varied than the mass culture theorists ever dreamt of. Individuals and groups respond differently and creatively to a range of inputs, from music to style and fashion, from adverts to film and TV. Each of our sections has marked balances and limits in the way these things are creatively taken up and used. But one finding insistently presents itself through all our work: the absolute centrality of the cultural media and commodities produced for the market. We have to conclude that, in general, the public sector can't do better than the commercial sector in supplying attractive and usable symbolic resources.

There is no point in hopeless competitions with the market, still less in desperate youth inoculations against it. Indeed, it is one of our base line positions that all of us are creative cultural consumers before we are cultural producers and that often these things merge in the play of everyday aesthetics. But it is as consumers that we must first be addressed. Widened, deepened and more creative consumption of commercially cultural commodities could be the motor for all kinds of desirable cultural ends. This is not to deny that there are sharp questions to be asked about the role of commerce and especially of multi-national corporations in the production of cultural commodities - their exploitation of workers and artists, their cupidity and avaricious guardianship of what they call 'software', their suppressions and distortions of cultural communication. But state subsidised and other sponsored forms of independent production will not dent this nexus of power. Expanded consumption, however, might produce new kinds of, and possibilities for, cultural production in general - some small part of which might result in successful entrepreneurial commercial forms or alternative collective forms of production, distribution and consumption. For the moment cultural production amongst young people remains fettered by their lack of access to, and control of, the widest possible range of usable symbolic resources. They're overpriced and overburdened with royalties, aimed at and marketed for those with 'cash demand' rather than for need in general.

By now we hope to have established in the reader's mind two linked and dominant cultural tendencies: 1. the unexpected life and promise of everyday grounded aesthetics in the ordinary life activities of young people; 2. articulated, surprisingly for some, for the most part through the popular cultural products and media of the mainly commercial market. At this point we would normally be expected to make firm proposals, such as recommending detailed policies aimed at limiting, directing or reinforcing these tendencies. Our policy aim is, indeed, to further reinforce and enable these tendencies, but we don't intend to make firm proposals. To begin with, such proposals are nearly always for new *institutions*. The point of what we have written is that traditional institutional forms are already numerous enough and don't work particularly well with the young, bar a small minority. Moreover, making detailed recommendations for existing organisations to act upon assumes that we know the constraints (historical, human, financial) which govern them with the intricacy and intimacy which they alone possess. It is for them to assess whether, from the field studies and ideas in this report, there is or is not something they can use, creatively, in their own way in their own circumstances.

In the case before us the means to desirable ends cannot simply be reached down from the conventional historical shelf of intervention and institution. The tendencies we have identified reflect too on any potential institutional means of control or direction. Much of the cultural creativity we have identified would evaporate when transferred to institutions. Many of the real symbolic energies of young people are essentially *informal* in their logic, meaning and motivation. We cannot clamp a *formal* template over this activity and expect the same meanings even to survive, never mind develop. Furthermore the creativities we've uncovered have developed precisely against the back-cloth of institutional failure or irrelevance. The nineteenth century cultural institutions which we have inherited have failed to provide for most young people a range of usable symbolic resources for their everyday cultural development. It will not do again to say, 'more of the same'.

Partly seriously, partly as devil's advocate, partly to signpost boldly and to experimentally press through the implications of our line of argument, we'd like, for a moment, to explore a different and irreverent view. We hear all the time of post-industrialism, post-modernism, post-feminism, even post-capitalism. Is it time now to speak also of 'post-institutionalism'? - that is, the recognition that institutions may be increasingly irrelevant to current needs, or indeed may do more unintentioned damage than intentioned good, and that new policy initiatives need to find quite new, much more indirect, less structured, more democratic, means for their execution. If existing institutions do not work, i.e. do not attract, then they should not be artificially propped up or multiplied no matter how high-minded they may be. Everything that can reasonably be left to the individual or small group should be. Cultural provision should be supplied through a multiplicity of providers. These providers should be of the mimimum practical size and enjoy no privileged guarantee of their survival beyond that of expressed popular demand for their services.

Institutions can be seen, in essence, as the attempt by one group *with power* (formerly through aristocratic patronage, now state patronage) to tell another larger group what is good for them: not to make their choices wider, but to make their choices *for* them. Although a self-congratulatory ethos often pervades social and cultural institutions, the truth may be that the complacency arises from fulfilling their own priorities rather than those of their clients. The identity-making and meaning-making activities of common culture have engulfed and gone beyond the cultural scope of our inherited institutions. Crudely: cultural institutions and cultural policy-makers can no longer pretend to know better than the style, fashion, media and music industries what young people want. Young people anyway chose from these commercial offerings in unforeseeable and informal ways. It may even be time simply to speak of the informal cultures of the young as their very own kind of sui generis 'thing' which no clapped on, or 'top-down' institution will ever make an impact on, except perhaps negatively.

For a balanced view it is necessary to step back a little from this devil's advocacy. We nevertheless believe that 'post-institutionalism' is a most useful base line of argument, to start from, keep in mind, and return to at moments of difficulty or indecision. However, it is too simplistic and too individualistic. It seems to indicate an overall public policy stance of benign neglect or of laissez-faire. The argument needs qualifying in a number of ways. Though the post-institutional scenario might be seductive in its boldness, it is in some essential respects a blatant kind of idealism.

Institutions exist, and will continue to exist. They are historically produced and are part of the social and cultural fabric of our existing and of any imaginable society. To deny their role may be simply to allow a continuing role for the wrong kinds of institutions.

It is, for instance, important to recognise that there is no such thing as an entirely 'free market' or 'free markets'. Markets and certainly the 'free enterprise' organisations which supply them for profit are institutions in their own rights - conditioned in many important respects by contents, structures and limits provided by multi-faceted aspects of the state and of state policy. Different parts of the state provide all kinds of hidden subsidies to the cultural market and its producers: zero VAT rating for printing; the provision of workers, skills and ideas through the education/training sector; the provision of that whole economic and social infra-structure which is the pre-condition for the running of any business large or small. The point might be to try to recognise these limits and to use whatever effectively they might offer for the furtherance of the cultural interests of the young.

How, in particular, would we qualify the 'laissez-faire' argument in cultural matters? First of all, with respect to that strand of our argument concerning the market provision of symbolic resources, we would want to point out that whilst market provision may have enabled cultural creativity it also maldistributes or only partially distributes cultural goods and technologies. Cash power is the arbiter of whether cultural needs are met or developed. As a mechanism this may well be more responsive, flexible and effective than a class of officials or institutions making the decisions, but it is far from perfect. There is a clear need for some redistributive supplement to the market to allow demands to be expressed and met even though they may not have 'cash power'. This is already a pressing issue for the vast army of unemployed or low paid young workers, but it is likely to become so, in differing ways, for the whole of youth as the 'youth market' declines or collapses (6).

There is also a continuing role for institutions to provide what cannot be provided by the market, but for which there will always be some demand. For instance, the market might fail to find an incentive for preserving for current use the symbolic products, materials and artefacts from the past which might otherwise be lost or otherwise not available. Paintings, writings, makings from all periods should be available to current cultural and symbolic work. For this there need to be institutions of safe-keeping. Furthermore the market tends towards replication and making more available what already exists and for which there is a predictable demand. There's certainly a case for short-span institutional initiatives to function almost as a kind of sponsored market research to test new ideas, to test different kinds of demand, their depth and persistence. There might also be something to be said for the state to acquire interests in copyright material by the provision of full compensation to the creators and other owners of such interests so as to release texts, performances and reproductions into the public domain.

The point might be to make these institutions as flexible and as non-hierarchical as possible, to follow a remit of maintaining and maximising access to the widest possible range of usable symbolic resources, rather than to pre-order or pre-value them according to internal, institutional value systems. Their aims, ideology and practical functioning should be as open, democratic and informal as possible.

We would also argue that the 'laissez-faire' option is faulted with respect to the other main strand of our argument concerning informal cultural creativity. In many important ways we live much of our current lives necessarily in the forms of the past. We're surrounded by, and live in, institutions set up at different times for purposes relevant to their times, energised by passions and possibilities of, designed against the limits of, their times - including the generally accepted norms of what was possible and passable. Though informal creativity may be organised in reaction to formality it is not without institutional aspects governed by the continuing reality of these institutions. Very often informal creativity occurs on sites - schools, clubs, dance-halls - and with materials organised or provided by institutions, and institutions which, one way or another, will persist into the foreseeable future. This raises the question of the type and form of institution and of the ways in which varieties of them might interact with, allow or disallow informal activity. For in the continuance of institutions can be change. The survival of institutions does not exclude the possibility of adaption. The direction of that change can be thought out and cumulatively resolved in consistent directions informed by some dialectical knowledge of the current of change outside the institutional walls.

Many organisational features of a wide variety of existing cultural institutions could be modified, or adjusted, to enable the possibility of creative informal symbolic work. Insofar as this is an accepted aim, then attention needs to be paid to the conditions under which creative cultural consumption is likely to take place. Our report suggests that these conditions concern informality, privacy, personal choice, power over, and access to, usable cultural commodities and resources.

The basic, if paradoxical, dynamic of change towards these ends might be thought of as an attempt to 'de-institutionalise' institutions and to 'de-centre' centres. This involves thinking about and applying 'openness' and 'design informality', providing, for instance, protected 'warm' spaces for sociability and communication. It means staffing and 'interfacing' by young people whenever possible and giving them the maximum scope of feasible power including consulting on design, organisation, appearance and human reception systems. It means experimenting with a variety of ways in which young people, if not enjoying formal ownership of cultural commodities and technologies, might nevertheless enjoy some kind of psychological ownership which encourages free, guiltless use. It means providing choice and variety in activities, space, hardware and software to the limits of practibility.

The high arts in particular need to be more available - in their practical conditions of material, social and psychological access - to informality and to the creative informal meanings of symbolic work. The success of Centerprise and Strongwords community writing projects show that, in certain situations, traditional forms can be chosen by non-elite groups to express direct and powerful informal symbolic meanings. The recent successes of certain museums and art galleries in appealing to more people and communicating with new audiences, and the continuing success of many libraries in providing an ever wider range of symbolic materials rest not on extending an old idea to 'new people', but in allowing 'new' people and their informal meanings and communications to colonise them, the institutions. Clearer and more focused thinking could re-inforce and greatly extend some of these already visible tendencies towards openness. Trusts and foundations have a clear role to play in supporting experiments aimed at shifting practices in this direction.

The institutional and organisational forms which supply the conditions and help to determine the possibilities, and type, of informal cultural creativity stretch much more widely, of course, than the institutions of direct cultural provision. It's difficult to draw the line here, and we suggest and prod rather than recommend. There is also a particular danger of the expedient attachment of cultural policy to other kinds of policy simply as a form of social control to keep young people out of trouble. Nevertheless we do believe that the desire to promote the everyday aesthetics and informal cultural creativity of the young, through the provision of conducive conditions, could have a very important influence on a variety of policy debates.

Whatever form of organisation and regulation of the media emerges over the next ten years, it seems essential to establish the principle of representation by young people in decision-making about programme-making - and not just of 'youth programming' but of programming in general - to ensure that the widest range of symbolic resources and forms are available and that programmed materials - irrespective of whether they are produced by or for young people - should be open, reflexive, and capable of supporting and encouraging the symbolic work of viewers. This need not be in the old fashioned way of 'worthy consultation'. As markets and audiences fragment it might make economic, as well as cultural, sense to involve young people in decision-making. Of course there will be many young people of low spending power who have little to interest programme-makers in them. Representation will have to include their interests in maintaining access to the widest range of programming which does not have to be paid for via subscription. At local level a variety of agencies should work to build a series of audio-visual spaces which provide the maximum possible range of open symbolic resources for young people's appropriation and use as well as access to all screen-based technologies.

Educational institutions are and will be in tension with the grounded aesthetics of the common culture of the young in a variety of ways. Whether this will be a positive or negative tension depends on how education develops. Common cultural forms, in one way or another, accompany young people into the classroom every day of their lives. For many young people they may be a more profound influence on their sense of self, identity and possibility than is the formal curriculum. Compulsory foundation subjects up to 16 in the national curriculum include music and the visual arts. What are these to be? What relationship might they have to common culture? The way in which the traditional arts continue to form the basis of the arts curriculum does not bode well here. The common culture of the young will certainly be there *informally*. It may creep into classroom practice as ways of keeping kids quiet by feeding and doping them up with popular cultural forms. Despite Queen being an option in GCSE, the usual use of pop music is still to play it simply to 'keep the kids quiet' on rainy afternoons. But this is the worst form of back door 'bread and circuses'.

More important than cynically taking over the contents of 'popular culture' would be a principled and thought out adoption of aspects of the processes and practices of the active *common* culture of the young: informal, democractic forms; symbolic creativity; the recognition and enablement of everyday aesthetics. If the arts curriculum continues to draw mostly from the 'high arts' of Western culture, more hopeful contacts with, and uses of, common cultural forms may arise in other areas. Media education classes, for instance, have often explored advertising, popular music, family photography and television drama. This could be much expanded. It may even be that extra-curricular and voluntary forms of activity might make the best cultural bridges into young peoples' actual cultural activities, with concrete musical, visual, style projects organised outside the school timetable and possibly at different sites.

Universities have traditionally provided cultural resources for the middle classes and the space and time to enjoy them. Further and Higher Education is due for expansion, with figures of up to 30% participation by the end of the century being suggested. What is certain is that Further and Higher Education is going to change and must recruit from social and economic groups which have not hitherto participated beyond school. Shouldn't Polytechnics and Colleges do far more than they do at present to become cultural centres and resources? And shouldn't the cultural resources they provide reflect the cultural interests of their students?

In lower level training generally, but especially for the cultural industries, we would argue for much more imaginative policies to be predicated on the recognition of the informal cultural productions of young people. Programmes could aim to develop informal symbolic work and creativity from their own bases as practical forms of training. Despite some exceptions, it remains in general the case that YTS is based on training for disappearing nineteenth century manual skills. Why not aim to base schemes on concrete cultural projects and activities? Why not develop assessment of, and credit for, practical skills and experience gained by young people on their own cultural projects? Artists, performers, professionals and business people could be asked to repay some of their hidden subsidies by giving their own time and expertise to youth projects in cultural production of various kinds.

There are already a number of music projects in major towns and cities which aim to provide young people with training in musical technique and, in some cases, with a wider range of business and management skills. These are intended to enable bands to set up and survive on local circuits and to produce and mix tapes for demonstration and sale. Realistically, the great majority of these bands will not 'make it' but for a period of time young musicians can be helped with the disciplines and skills to perform and develop musically. Arguably, the experience of succeeding within a local musical scene, the skills and attitudes learned in the process, the opportunity to work with other people to translate ideas into successful projects are all crucial parts of the transition from youth into adulthood. There is a real argument for more funding to go to such projects: the Arts Council still does not fund pop music.

Training based on cultural activities is almost non-existent. Yet this may be what young people are interested in. Why does training have to be linked to such narrow vocational aims as it is at present? Why shouldn't young people have the opportunity for a wider and richer diet of training which offers the chance to develop creative and expressive abilities and technical and personal skills? Such training could feed back into young people's cultural lives as well as helping them acquire a range of useful transferable skills on which specific job training could later be built. This emphasis within training should challenge the narrow vocationalism of the present with an open vocationalism which looks to the development of the individual in general. There is enough evidence of the failure of our current training policies to make this a powerful strand of future thinking.

Many of our cities are in danger of collapse socially and economically. Public space is being eradicated, housing has been removed, shopping malls are dirty, dull and shut up after dark, the young unemployed are the new pariahs unwanted and shunted around by private security guards. Too often the assumption is made that it is the inner city dwellers who are the problem. But the pressing needs for inner city revitalisation will only be met in and by the release of the talents and energies of the young and other people who live in the inner city. Why not start some new projects from the premise that all young people are their own kinds of cultural producer, and apply state subsidies, services and 'pump priming' to these existing human and symbolic resources?

There are a lot of possibilities here. The idea - from Sheffield and Wolverhampton - of creating entertainment zones where venues and facilities are concentrated to create a 'Covent Garden Market' effect is of great interest. This would help to create local night-time economies - live music, clubs, cafes, bars, late night shops - and provide clean, well-lit places for young people to go as well as places to work in. It would bring life back into centres and create a sense of local ownership.

In working through such possibilities for imaginative developments in a range of local policies and institutions it would be important to involve Local Authority services and especially youth related services in new kinds of ways. The Youth Service, for instance, is still by and large operating along traditonal lines in its philosophy of social and informal education and the provision of conventional youth clubs and opportunities for protected forms of socialisation. It could, however, operate in a much broader and more 'arm's length' kind of way, and with a much broader remit with an older age group in mind, to act as the enabler and co-ordinator of the youth dimension of many of the initiatives and ideas suggested here. In particular it might focus on the encouragement of youth autonomy and the control of assets and resources by and for young people themselves as specific contributions in particular areas to cultural development and emancipation in general (7).

These points have dealt with possible changes of direction within some of the existing 'macro' institutions, agencies and organisations which we have inherited and which will, in whatever form, continue to set many of the conditions under which informal cultural creativity occurs. But we would argue that it is mistaken to assume that informal cultural activity is itself without institutional dimensions - real, possible or immanent. Young people must take their own time on their own territory with their own familiar meanings to arrive at what is needed and necessary in their cultural creativity, but this does not preclude some formality of organisation in what is needed. The problem arises, in part, from our own sombre institutional view of institutions, their proper atmosphere, functions and purposes. Not only new institutions, but new and broader views of what institutions are, might be or become, and of how institutions might form and evolve are needed for the fullest promotion and development of active cultural citizens under modern conditions.

There are, in fact, what we might call informal institutions within informal cultural life: communities and collectivities which connect individuals and are larger than their simple sum. Insubstantial, shifting, combining, atrophying, recombining, they start not from intentioned purposes but from contingency, from shared desires, from decentred overlaps, from accidents. The form, unplanned and unorganised, out of patterns in shared symbolic work and creativity. Such informal communities may involve direct communication around a 'consuming interest' (listening, dancing, talking) in certain types of music or in a variety of ways of producing music. They may arise in eclectic combinations of consumers who discover, incidentally, that they share a taste or interest as they meet in friendship, neighbourhood, school or work place groups. But informal communities may also be 'serial'. These are social groupings not connected through direct communication but through shared styles, fashions, interests, empathies, positions and passions - sometimes shared simultaneously 'off-air' through the communication media. Metaphorically, a 'serial community' is a spaced out queue of people rather than a talking circle. The same person, or bits of them, may simultaneously be in several such 'queues'. But they are still placed more than randomly or chaotically in social and material place and time, and can, therefore, sometimes make or be made a living circle if time and place co-incide because of the essential *social* connectedness of informal work and creativity. Informal communities may also arise in one-off celebrations of the sensuousness of, and sheer fun possible in the collectivity of mass events such as Live-Aid and Comic Relief.

Where the earnestness of the old intentionality produces boredom and disaffection, informal communities grow from self- direction, from what gives pleasure, satisfies or promotes desire, from 'fun', from the *shared* passions of what really motivates and energises individuals.

Out of these informal communities young people do sometimes consciously organise themselves and make demands: for their own kinds of formal institutions; for autonomous self-organisation; for 'arm's length' funding; for their own more formal control of activities, provision and use of resources.

Often youth demands arise from, in the first instance, having been given a 'little' on a provided base but which nevertheless shows the possibilities for openness and self-organisation. The 'success' of such provision may then be greeted, not with thanks, but with doubled or new demands.

The highly interesting point here is that when young people *do* make demands and seek to self-organise, their interests and demands run almost always along a cultural dynamic. This dynamic arises from informal passions and energies and focuses on the need for much greater access to, and control of, relevant symbolic materials and cultural assets. Imaginative 'venue campaigns' have been conducted in Norwich - spontaneously organised groups of young people campaigning for music performance and cultural centres to be designed and controlled by them. The Waterfront project in Norwich now has premises and a budget running into hundreds of thousands of pounds. A similar successful campaign was organised in Telford resulting in the establishing of a young people's 'Culture Centre'. In the early 80s in Wolverhampton a group of Rasterfarians sat outside the Council Chamber in Wolverhampton refusing to move until the Council Leader came to talk to them. Finally he did just that and promised them funds for their own centre which subsequently became the base for the Wolverhampton Rastafarian Progressive Association organising its own sound systems, workshops and education classes.

Though agencies of various kinds may not be able to initiate such movements, they can certainly think about and try to promote some of the general conditions which are most likely to produce self-organisation and demands from below. They can certainly respond positively and constructively to demands once made and provide 'arm's length' funding and support. They can also strive to keep to an absolute minimum the restrictive conditions - relating perhaps to the need to respect others' freedom to pursue their own cultural development - in their grant-giving roles and functions.

There are no guarantees, of course, that all autonomous self-organised youth bodies would function or survive. Policy would have explicitly to recognise risk and place 'risk umbrellas' over projects expecting a certain proportion of them to fail. Who is to say that youth institutions should last forever? This is to invite the tyranny of youth gerontocracies suppressing new generations. In youth affairs, particularly, we should not expect permanence. Permanence is no proof that we have found a solution. Often the reverse. Often it is what leads institutions into their false pursuit of monuments, organisational and material, as ways of trying to compensate for or defeat the ephemeral nature of human experience. But we should encourage *process and practice* not *product*. We should welcome and expect 'fire and phoenix' as regular features of youth organisation life. But still there is an important institutional and organisational dimension which should not be overlooked.

The voluntary sector and the foundations, especially in the current climate, may have a particularly important role to play in setting new directions and encouraging an atmosphere of confidence in youth's own self-activity as cultural producers. In many aspects of openness; psychological ownership; self-direction; the separation between providers and paymasters; the separation between providers and authority state institutional forms may have much to learn from voluntary organisation and from 'arm's length' forms of funding.

We have eschewed the opportunity to outline detailed designs for further 'top-down' solutions and institutions for the cultural realm. Our main hope is that the arguments in this report will be taken up and addressed by people in their own fields: the media; education and training; town planning; youth and arts providers and so on. We don't have magic wands to give to these people, nor do we pretend to know better than them their own practical business. New ideas must grow in their own soil. But we would like to end with an example of one firm proposal for reasonable action that flows from our analysis. The development of fully formed, autonomous cultural citizens is our goal. It may help, however, to make this possibility palpable in some identifiable way.

The idea is this: that a handful of local independent cultural trusts - perhaps called *The X Cultural Exchange* depending on locality -

should be set up, possibly in association with local authorities, funded from a variety of sources including foundations as well as from private industry. Such trusts would have two principal aims: 1. to help enhance the power of freely chosen creative *cultural consumption*, especially amongst young people with no 'cash power' on the market; 2. to help enhance the possibility of the development of multiple, independent and autonomous, 'arm's length' sites and organisations of cultural provision and activity, especially through the creation and encouragement of self-directed, autonomous youth organisations.

The mechanism for promoting these aims would be in the provision of a local 'cultural currency'. Individual 'notes of cultural exchange' would be issued to individuals who could use them to be exchanged against a stated cash value of cultural commodities or services, use of equipment or space. Suppliers of such commodities, services or assets - from theatres and art galleries, to music shops, to local authority leisure departments supplying recording facilities or sound proofed studios - would simply redeem for cash the notes they take in at the local cultural trust. Collective 'notes of cultural exchange' might also be issued or lent under minimal conditions to self-organised voluntary groups, especially those attempting to pioneer new ideas for provision or activity. Collective 'notes of cultural exchange' would also be exchanged for set amounts of commodities, services or assets necessary to the setting up of new organisations. Holders of individual 'notes' would also be able 'spontaneously' to combine their currency to form organisations of cultural activity or provision as they wished or saw fit. All these organisations would, in turn, be able to take in individual notes of cultural exchange and redeem them for cash at the cultural trust.

Either the local cultural trust directly or one of the cultural providers it helps to float off could also set up an institutional form to explore the barter potentials of cultural exchange whereby records, CDs, instruments, hardware etc might be swapped between individuals directly with no 'commercial' or 'cultural currency' involvement at all.

Both cultural exchange and the cultural barter ideas would be more likely to succeed if there were good and widespread local publicity and an *internal* connection with locally-based cultural media. Synergics between local cultural practices/initiatives and local media forms/ contents have hardly been explored. The likely rapid emergence of cable TV as an aspect of the forthcoming 'TV revolution' might offer real opportunities here.

Apart from simple and minimal guidelines, local cultural trusts would place no value or restriction on particular cultural forms, materials or activities, nor would they expect 'success', seek to ensure or control it. They would simply act as the issuer and redeemer of the local cultural currency.

Frankly experimental? Yes. We don't know what, and if, new kinds of institutions and activities might develop from local cultural trusts. We do know that new, open, more flexible thinking and organisation is required if we mean to cherish, rather than ignore and flatten, the everyday aesthetics which, as we have tried to show, richly pervade the lives of young people.

Some Questions for the General Reader

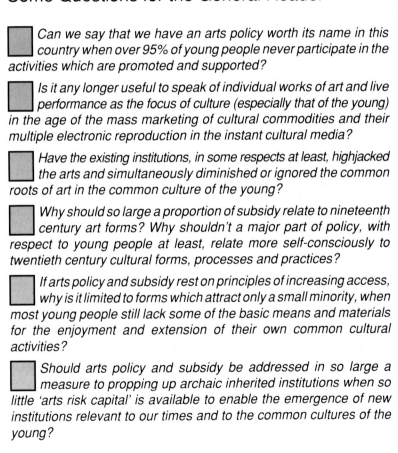

Can we say that we have an arts policy worth its name in this country when over 95% of young people never participate in the activities which are promoted and supported?

Is it any longer useful to speak of individual works of art and live performance as the focus of culture (especially that of the young) in the age of the mass marketing of cultural commodities and their multiple electronic reproduction in the instant cultural media?

Have the existing institutions, in some respects at least, highjacked the arts and simultaneously diminished or ignored the common roots of art in the common culture of the young?

Why should so large a proportion of subsidy relate to nineteenth century art forms? Why shouldn't a major part of policy, with respect to young people at least, relate more self-consciously to twentieth century cultural forms, processes and practices?

If arts policy and subsidy rest on principles of increasing access, why is it limited to forms which attract only a small minority, when most young people still lack some of the basic means and materials for the enjoyment and extension of their own common cultural activities?

Should arts policy and subsidy be addressed in so large a measure to propping up archaic inherited institutions when so little 'arts risk capital' is available to enable the emergence of new institutions relevant to our times and to the common cultures of the young?

Some Questions for the Specialist Reader

Are the creative activities and everyday aesthetics of young people's common culture fully recognised in your own thinking and in the practices of institutions of which you may be part?

Is the rigid separation of production and consumption in cultural matters the historical norm or itself the aberration? Can we learn from youth's common culture how to encourage creative production of all kinds through creative consumption? How can we further develop youth's creativity by freeing up access to the widest range of cultural items, resources and material?

Are all avenues and sources of influence thoroughly explored in order to exert downward pressure on the price of cultural commodities and resources, and so to increase popular access and use? Should financial support be aimed more at subsidising or buying out interests in copyright by the provision of fair compensation for the creators and/or other owners of those interests at the date of sale, thus cheapening commodities for the majority rather than making live performance cheaper for minorities?

How can the traditional institutions be opened up and developed in ways more consonant with the terms of youth's common culture and aimed at developing its informal activities and aesthetics?

How can major areas of policy, practice and institution - in the media, in local authority services, in education and training, in urban regeneration and in the encouragement of night-time economies - learn from, and seek to encourage, the creative informal cultures of the young within their own domains?

What 'arm's length' initiatives, policies or practices might allow for and encourage more organised activities to emerge from the informal activities and collectivities of youth's common culture?

What imaginative initiatives, such as The Cultural Exchange idea, can and might be developed to supplement market provision of cultural commodities and resources in order to equalise access to and free up the 'convertability' of cultural resources?

Notes

1 Definitions are always hazardous but we mean here something like the officially supported and/or institutionalised practices of literature, theatre, ballet, opera, fine art and museums.

2 *Cultural Trends 1989*, No 2, Policy Studies Institute. The figures quoted in this text refer to visits undertaken in the four weeks prior to interview date. The sample size was 1902. The General Household Survey figures are regarded as generally the most reliable from a variety of not very adequate statistical sources.

As we go to press the results of the *1987 General Household Survey* have been published (January 1990). This shows a small but noticeable upwards movement in arts attendance figures. 'Plays, pantomimes or musicals' recorded 7% participation, 'Classical music' 2%, with 1% each for 'Ballet or modern dance' and 'Operas or operettas'. 'Art galleries or museums' recorded 8% - double the 1986 figure. Social class differences persist with between 3-4% of the working class attending 'Plays, pantomimes or musicals', 1% 'Classical music', with under 1% attending 'Ballet or modern dance' and 0% 'Opera or operettas'. Around 5% attend 'Art galleries or museums'.

It is surprising that these changes, however small, should be recorded after many years of absolute consistency. However, it should be noted that the *1987 General Household Survey* for the first time adopted a partially different definition of arts activities and also utilised a different methodology for the administration of the relevant question on the questionnaire. This raises the possibility that the higher figures might be an artefact of research method rather than a reflection of reality.

Opera was dropped from the 'Theatre/ballet/opera' category, the balance of which was re-formed and expanded into 'Plays, pantomimes or musicals (including folk, rock or pop concerts)'. Whereas in 1986 and before respondents were asked to volunteer their activities, in the 1987 survey they were given a checklist of items to mark off with a very full explanatory gloss for 'Art galleries or museums': 'public and private, in historic buildings (e.g. Beaulieu Motor Museum, Ham House), museums attached to archeological sites, open air museums'.

The most recent survey evidence (reported in *The Times*, 9/10/89) compiled by the British Market Research Bureau for the Arts Council and based on an average period of four weeks during 1988-89 lends some support to the view that attendance rates have increased but on a much shallower trend than suggested by the *1987 General Household Survey*. They found that 6% of the adult population went to the theatre, 4% to an art gallery and 2% to classical music.

3 P Willis et al, *The Youth Review,* Avebury 88. Survey questions referred to activities undertaken in the prior seven days.

4 See McRobbie A and Garber, J. (1975) 'Girls and Subcultures': An Exploration in S Hall and T Jefferson (eds), *Resistance Through Rituals: Youth Culture in Post-war Britain,* London Hutchinson.

5 *General Household Survey, 1983,* P Willis et al. *The Youth Review,* 1988.

6 The Henley Centre for Forecasting (1986) predicts that this collapse will be brought on by the decline in numbers of young adults (24% decline in 15-24 year-olds by 1996), continuously high levels of youth unemployment and rising levels of real disposable income among other segments of the population. They forecast that products and services will be restyled or introduced and marketed to rising market groups: young family groupings among 25-44 year-olds, as well as 'empty-nester' groups among 45-59 years-old.

7 See *The Youth Review,* op cit, for an extended discussion of how local authority services might be generally re-directed and reorganised along the lines of a 'Youth Affairs' rather than a 'Youth Service' perspective.

Appendix

Commissioned Studies

Title:	*Fashion and the Clothing Industry*
Author:	Juliette Ash

Title:	*The Cultural Responses of Young People to Unemployment*
Author:	Labour Market Studies Group, University of Leicester (Dave Ashton and Malcolm Macquire)

Title:	*Facts About Culture*
Author:	Ian Connell

Title:	*Young People and Music*
Author:	Simon Frith

Title:	*Music Activity in South Birmingham; Style and Fashion in Young People's Lives*
Author:	Simon Jones

Title:	*A Study of Youth Art Policies*
Author:	Celia Lury

Title:	*Young Women, Second-hand Clothes and Style*
Author:	Angela McRobbie

Title:	*Black Hair/Style Politics*
Author:	Kobena Mercer

Title:	*Young People and Communications Technologies; Implications for Creativity*
Author:	Graham Murdock

Title:	*TV Commercials and Young People*
Authors:	Mica and Orson Nava

Title: *Young People and Video*
Author: Dead Honest Sole Searchers (Graham Peat)

Title: *The Young Consumer - Commercial
Strategies and Young People's
Everyday Activity in Britain
1950-1990; Voluntary Activity,
Public Policy and the Cultural
Activity of Young People*
Author: Alan Tomlinson

Title: *Creative Identity: The Role of
Fantasy in the Everyday Life of the Young
Unemployed*
Author: Derek Walsgrove

Title: *Young People and Sport*
Author: Gary Whannel

Title: *Young People and Magazine Culture*
Author: Janice Winship